ROCK CLIMBING ANCHORS
A Comprehensive Guide

MOUNTAINEERS
OUTDOOR EXPERT
series

ROCK CLIMBING ANCHORS
A Comprehensive Guide

Topher Donahue and Craig Luebben

Second edition

MOUNTAINEERS
BOOKS

This book is dedicated to everyone who believes that walls are for climbing.

MOUNTAINEERS BOOKS is dedicated to the exploration, preservation, and enjoyment of outdoor and wilderness areas.

1001 SW Klickitat Way, Suite 201, Seattle, WA 98134
800-553-4453, www.mountaineersbooks.org

Printed in China
Distributed in the United Kingdom by Cordee, www.cordee.co.uk

First edition, 2007. Second edition, 2019.

Copyeditor: Erin Cusick
Design and layout: McKenzie Long
Cover photograph: *Patience Gribble being careful not to take a factor-2 fall onto the belay anchor during the first ascent of* Cameron's Pillar *(5.11 +), South Howser Tower, Bugaboos, British Columbia*
Frontispiece: *Alex Honnold treading the fine line between fun and danger in the Elbsandstein, Germany, on a pitch with only five pieces of gear in 50 meters*
Photographers: Craig Luebben and Topher Donahue
Illustrator: Jeremy Collins

Library of Congress Cataloging-in-Publication data is on file for this title at
https://lccn.loc.gov/2018050955

Mountaineers Books titles may be purchased for corporate, educational, or other promotional sales, and our authors are available for a wide range of events. For information on special discounts or booking an author, contact our customer service at 800-553-4453 or mbooks@mountaineersbooks.org.

Printed on FSC®-certified materials

ISBN (paperback): 978-1-68051-140-6
ISBN (ebook): 978-1-68051-141-3

An independent nonprofit publisher since 1960

Contents

Opposite: *Vera Schulte-Pelkum entering the fun zone where the ground is far enough below that falls are safe and soft on* Not My Cross to Bear *(5.11), Penitente Canyon, Colorado*

Introduction

Climbing has always been a fascinating amalgamation of romantic adventure; a nerdy, science-experiment-like endeavor; and a physical, athletic pursuit. Craig Luebben, the author of the first edition of this book, was gifted in communicating all three of these seemingly disparate aspects of the sport. Thanks to climbing gyms and the social media culture, modern climbing tends to be seen as more athletic than scientific or adventurous, and as such, Craig's books may be more useful than ever before. When we're getting pumped on a sport climb or checking out the instatweet-chatbook feeds showing fit climbers after their latest send, it's easy to forget the basic forces that make the sport both beautiful and dangerous. Craig, a scientist by training, introduced the first edition with a fundamental reminder of what makes climbing work:

Gravity: The tireless force that pulls two bodies together. The more massive the bodies and the closer they are, the stronger the pull. Earth's huge mass creates an enormous gravitational force that traps the atmosphere, holds the planet together, drives glaciers and rivers, and makes climbing what it is—fun and challenging, yet sometimes frightening, perilous, and hard. Gravity lurks and lingers, always ready to pluck a climber from her tenuous stance. When a climber does fall, it's up to the rope and anchors to catch her.

Climbing anchors allow us to "safely" defy gravity. We use them to build belay and rappel stations, set top ropes, and protect lead climbers. Solid anchors and proper rope techniques can prevent a fall from turning into a catastrophe; bad anchors are an accident waiting to happen.

Setting anchors is simple and straightforward on many climbs; on other routes, finding the anchors and engineering the protection system can be a significant part of the climb's challenge. For some climbers, the problem-solving aspect of creating anchors is one of the many appeals of rock climbing. For others, setting anchors is just a duty to keep the climbing safe. Either way, having a large repertoire of anchoring techniques makes climbing safer and more efficient.

This perspective is perhaps even more important now than it was when Craig first wrote it, because the number of people who need to learn the fundamentals of how climbing anchors work has grown exponentially since then, and most climbers today are introduced to the sport in the seemingly safe environment of the climbing gym. For this reason, one of the big additions to this second edition is a chapter on climbing gym anchors (see chapter 8). For experienced rock climbers, the concept of climbing gym anchors may seem like an oxymoron, but think again. In this book, *anchor* means anything that attaches a climber to the wall, regardless of whether the wall is made of rock, concrete, or plywood. This includes the bolts; natural protection; and top-rope, lower-off, or belay anchors. Gravity works the same in the gym as it does outside, and the forces of swinging falls and climber location relative to the anchors and the belayer are equally applicable to indoor and outdoor climbing.

Some of the ideas and techniques presented here come from the guide's perspective; these are systems that are used day in, day out by thousands of guides around the world. Other information comes from the light-and-fast school, where speed, efficiency, and skill trump the urge to build big, complex belay anchors.

Many valid climbing styles, rope systems, and anchor-rigging techniques exist—there are dozens of ways to crack an egg. This is where creativity meets science. There are a lot of options for building an anchor; in the end it needs to be strong enough for the given situation and convenient to use. The key is to understand the potential forces and build anchors that can handle the forces with strength to spare, all while constructing the anchors quickly, cleanly, and without using excessive gear.

On opposite extremes, a team of intermediate climbers may set as many anchors in a four-pitch route as a speed team does in twenty pitches. The speed climbers are cutting corners where they feel climbing skill can compensate for safety protocol, using advanced rope techniques and increasing risk tolerance in order to achieve their goal of climbing *fast*. This variation among climbing teams is fine because everyone is (hopefully) having fun and accomplishing their objectives without mishap.

In the gym, climbers don't build anchors, but they certainly use them; probably more falls are now held by gym anchors than by anchors in real rock, and knowing when to clip, how to assess potential falls by both you and your partner as well as climbers around you, and how to take into account the difference in body weight between climber and belayer makes the difference between a great experience and an unpleasant, painful, and potentially dangerous one.

Most instructional books can be accused of encouraging protocol-based solutions to problems. But the climbing landscape is too complex and the variables too many to be served well by protocol. A climber needs the flexibility to craft a solution for each situation. Protocol is necessary for beginners and still important for intermediates. For anyone seeking to become a good climber, though, the best plan is to become educated and experienced, so you can consistently and quickly make good judgment-based decisions. The ultimate goal of this book is to help you on that quest.

Craig and I started climbing together when he was working on his engineering degree and I was in high school. We shared a common interest in not just making climbing safe enough, but in making it as safe as possible while still pushing our own athletic and adventure limits. I recall spending many hours on the long road trips between climbing areas discussing the myriad details and physics of climbing anchors. Craig was a great mentor for me, and I helped him to embrace the go-for-it attitude that has become so prevalent in the modern climbing culture. We climbed together in Canada, China, and all over the United States. After Craig's untimely death in 2009, his widow, Silvia, invited me to author this second edition.

While working on this book, I climbed in Eldorado Canyon with Craig's daughter, Giulia, who, at thirteen years old, was already climbing 5.13 in the gym. She hadn't done much hard traditional climbing, so we spent a day climbing the tenuous, naturally protected thin cracks that split the soaring arêtes of Eldorado's Redgarden Wall. Watching her solve the complex sequences, use anchors of her dad's invention—the Big Bro—and enjoy the airy belays and the birdlife soaring around us reminded me of my early days climbing, when I followed better and more-experienced climbers than I, including her dad. This part of learning to climb, the mentorship, is something that no book and not even the vast (and often misleading) information available on the internet can replace. Every climber will do well to find someone, a guide or friend, who can be your mentor and do for you what Craig did for me and what I have done for Giulia. Then, when you're the more experienced climber on the team and you've mastered everything in this book and more, do the same for your partner and help to pass on the love and lessons of this great sport.

How To Use This Book

The material presented here is important for any climber who uses anchors, from beginner to intermediate to advanced rock climbers, alpinists, and mountaineers. We assume the reader has basic climbing skills and knowledge, including belaying, communication signals, moving over rock, rappelling, top-roping, and lead climbing. Climbers lacking familiarity with these techniques may find *Rock Climbing: Mastering Basic Skills*, by this author, a better starting point.

Chapter 1 focuses on anchors for top-roping, rappelling, sport climbing, leading trad routes, and belay stations. It discusses the forces generated in a fall, how many pieces to set for an anchor, how V-angles can increase forces, how to build and equalize multidirectional anchors, how to attach yourself to anchors, belay techniques, and how to evaluate rock quality.

Chapter 2 covers natural anchors, such as trees, boulders, blocks, flakes, chockstones, horns, and threads, and fixed anchors, such as pitons and bolts. Chapter 3 discusses all types of chocks, including wired nuts, hex nuts, Tricams, sliding nuts, and Big

Bros. Chapter 4 examines cams, including how they evolved, how they work, how to place or remove them, and how to discern between good and bad placements.

The first four chapters provide the foundation for the anchor systems shown later in the book. Chapters 5–9 can stand alone— pick and choose the chapters that pique your climbing interests.

Chapter 5 discusses top-rope and rappel anchors, and chapter 6 talks about protecting sport climbs. Chapter 7 covers how to rig trad belay anchors using a cordelette, slings, or a climbing rope. Chapter 8 dives into the specifics of anchors in the climbing gym, with particular focus on managing fall trajectories by considering the interaction between the leader, the anchors, and the belayer. Chapter 9 explains considerations for protecting the lead on traditional routes. The final chapter explains how physics affects the forces in lead climbing falls, what types of falls are the most risky, and how to reduce the impact in high-force falls.

Appendix 1 discusses cords, webbing, and carabiners. The second appendix shows a variety of knots used for rigging anchor systems, and the third appendix includes equations for those who didn't get enough physics in chapter 10.

FURTHER TRAINING

Each climber in a team shares responsibility for keeping the team safe and self-reliant, and each must be knowledgeable about climbing anchors and rope work. If you always rely on your partners to take care of you, what will you do if they get hurt and need you to get the team up or down? Get professional instruction if you're a beginner or if you have glaring holes in your climbing knowledge.

Safe climbing requires good anchoring skills. This text covers many techniques, but it is still only a collection of words, photographs, and illustrations. Climbers seeking to develop their anchoring skills should take an intensive, on-the-rocks anchor clinic with an American Mountain Guides Association (AMGA) certified rock guide or a guide who works for an AMGA-accredited school. Material found on these pages will supplement such a course. Experienced climbers can use the book to fine-tune old techniques and learn some new ones.

Climbing gear and techniques are constantly evolving. Climbers of all experience levels should stay current by reading magazine and high-quality technique articles online and updated instructional manuals. Keep your eye out for product recalls, which happen all too frequently in the climbing industry.

ENVIRONMENTAL CONSIDERATIONS

Climbing has become so popular that many areas are being overrun. We have a duty to help preserve our climbing areas, to keep them beautiful and open to climbing. This means using trails and avoiding side paths and shortcuts; preventing damage to plants or trees; picking up trash (including tape scraps and cigarette butts) whether it is yours or not; minimizing the use of chalk tick marks and removing those marks when you're done; burying or carrying human waste (or better, settling these needs *before* going to the crag); minimizing noise; and keeping pets from chasing wildlife or annoying other climbers.

As the sport gains popularity and the number of climbers increases, human impact becomes a growing concern, maybe the biggest concern. Just as we monitor our anchors for security, we should monitor them for impact on the rock and the terrain around the cliff. Because of climbing's intimate relationship with the natural world, climbers can serve as a sort of canary in the coal mine of environmental impact. Alpine climbers will notice environmental changes the most due to the fragile characteristics of ice and snow, but rock climbers also notice changes in temperature, flora, and fauna.

Our product choices and travel habits also impact the environment. Many brands now support environmental initiatives and produce products that are less damaging to the environment and require less energy to produce. For example, a recent rope-making

Reducing human impact—by setting anchors to prevent these wear grooves while top-roping on soft sandstone, for example—should be a goal of every climber.

innovation reduces water consumption by 89 percent, energy consumption by 63 percent, carbon emissions by 62 percent, and chemical use by 63 percent compared to conventional climbing-rope production methods. The entire outdoor industry—even the traditionally separate cultures of climbing, hunting, fishing, skiing, four-wheeling, and others—is now finding itself on the same team in terms of preserving access and maintaining the quality of experience while minimizing human impact on our planet.

CLIMBING ORGANIZATIONS

Find contact information for the organizations listed here in the Resources section at the back of this book.

The **Access Fund** is a climbing advocacy group that promotes conservation and climbing access. Anyone who loves climbing should join the Access Fund to support its mission of keeping climbing areas open and promoting healthy stewardship of the land.

Leave No Trace promotes low-impact use of the outdoors and teaches responsible outdoor practices through its training programs.

The **International Climbing and Mountaineering Federation** (UIAA, Union Internationale des Associations d'Alpinisme) is a federation of ninety-seven national climbing and mountaineering associations from sixty-eight countries. UIAA supports all forms of climbing and mountaineering, encourages environmentally acceptable climbing practices, governs international climbing competitions, promotes cooperation and interaction among climbers from all nations, and seeks to minimize the hazards involved in climbing. The UIAA safety commission has created testing standards for climbing equipment to ensure that available gear is suitable for climbing. Gear must pass a battery of tests in a UIAA-approved testing laboratory to receive UIAA certification. When buying equipment, look for the UIAA safety label so you know that it passes UIAA standards.

The European Union (EU) has also created standards for climbing gear based on UIAA standards. Gear passing EU standards will be marked with a CE (Conformité Européene) label.

The **American Mountain Guides Association** (AMGA) is a nonprofit organization that trains and certifies guides in three disciplines—rock climbing, alpine climbing, and ski mountaineering. To become certified an individual guide must take courses, work with mentors, gain extensive climbing and guiding experience, and pass rigorous multiday field examinations.

A guide service or school can be accredited by AMGA after a review of its safety, training, and administrative practices. I recommend hiring AMGA-certified climbing guides or guides working for accredited services. Otherwise you may be wasting your money, your time, or worse.

WARNING! READ THE FOLLOWING BEFORE USING THIS BOOK

Climbing is dangerous. You can be killed or seriously injured while rock climbing. No book can describe or predict all the hazardous and complex situations that can occur while climbing, and the techniques described here are not appropriate for all climbing situations.

The information provided here is intended to supplement formal, competent instruction. Do not rely on this text as your primary source of rock climbing information—a simple misinterpretation could be disastrous. Climbing safely requires good judgment based on experience, competent instruction, and a realistic understanding of your personal skills and limitations. Even if you do everything right, you can still get injured or killed.

This book contains only the personal opinions of the authors, and it focuses exclusively on climbing anchors, so it lacks coverage of a great deal of important climbing safety techniques and procedures. The authors and publisher make no warranties, express or implied, that the information contained here is accurate or reliable. Further, the authors and publisher make no warranties as to fitness for a particular purpose or that this book is merchantable, and they assume no liability for readers who participate in any activities discussed here. Use of this text implies that you accept responsibility for your own climbing safety, and you assume the risk of injury or death.

—*Mountaineers Books*

Opposite: *Katie Frayler, Tiffany Junge, and Cassie Beermann enjoy their belay on Castle Rock, Colorado.*

CHAPTER 1

Anchor Basics

One of the beauties of rock climbing is its amazing diversity. Sea cliffs, high alpine faces, desert towers, water-carved canyons, random crags in the woods: the geographical possibilities are endless. Add in the different rock types: impeccable granite, wildly featured limestone, flawless sandstone, and myriad other igneous, metamorphic, and sedimentary rocks, ranging from choss to totally solid. You can also change the angle, from tip-toe friction slabs to striking vertical faces to gymnastic roofs and caves; or pick a crack of any size, from fingertips to chimneys. You can pursue boulder problems, eighty-foot sport routes, multipitch gear routes, or massive walls.

Then you have the protection factor, ranging from no-commitment top ropes to athletic clip-ups, and from splitter cracks that devour pro to dicey, runout, rarely climbed test pieces. And how much effort do you want to spend? You can choose from easy romps, full-throttle on-sights, and multiday redpoint projects. Given all this variety, one thing remains common: most rock climbing (besides bouldering and free soloing) relies on anchors for creating the safety system.

In this chapter, we'll discuss how anchors are used for

- top-roping,
- rappelling,
- sport climbing,
- leading traditional routes,
- multipitch belay stations.

Then we'll discuss

- what kind of forces can be generated in a fall;
- how many pieces to set in an anchor;
- how to build equalized, redundant anchors;
- avoiding large V-angles that amplify forces;
- creating multidirectional anchors;
- attaching yourself to the anchor with the rope, slings, or a daisy chain;
- pre-equalizing versus self-equalizing;
- using the appropriate belay technique;
- evaluating rock quality.

Timmy O'Neill makes good use of a top rope in the Calico Hills, Red Rock Canyon, Nevada.

TYPES OF CLIMBING ANCHORS

When climbers talk about "anchors," they are usually referring to critical transition points, such as the point where a sport climber finishes a pitch, the top of an indoor climbing wall, rappel and top-rope anchors, and the place where a team on a multipitch route stops to belay. For the purpose of this book, we define anchors as any anchor point on a climb. This includes protection—"pro"—placed midpitch; bolts permanently fixed on the cliff or in the gym; pitons; clean protection, such as nuts and cams; as well as terrain anchors, like trees or flakes.

TOP-ROPE ANCHORS

When top-roping, the rope usually runs from the climber up to anchors at the top of the route, then back down to the belayer. This setup is called a "slingshot" top rope. With the rope anchored above the climber, the belayer can immediately halt a fall, which makes top-roping one of the safest ways to climb. Depending on the situation, anchors can be set at the lip of the cliff or back from the edge and extended with slings or cord over the cliff edge.

In some cases, the climbing team may anchor the belayer atop the cliff. This setup works well if the base of the cliff is difficult to access or too tall for a slingshot

Jared Ogden rappelling into the Black Canyon of the Gunnison, Colorado

top rope. Chapter 5 explains how to rig the system whether the belayer is above or below the climb.

RAPPEL ANCHORS

If an established climb does not have a reasonable walk-off, it should have fixed rappel anchors for descending. You may want to set up a belay to look for them because they're not always easy to find. Fixed rappel anchors run the gamut from completely solid to totally sketchy—it's up to you to make sure you can trust the anchors with your life. Chapter 5 covers how to evaluate fixed rappel anchors, how to back them up, and how to rig rappel stations (to clean up messy stations or create new ones). It also explains much of the standard hardware found on cliffs.

LOWER-OFF ANCHORS

Most climbs are less than half a rope-length long and end at a permanently fixed anchor. When the leader reaches the top, she clips the anchor, signals to her belayer that she is ready to descend, and then weights the rope and is lowered back to the ground. It is during this transition that many accidents happen in climbing, and learning the basics as well as understanding that no two anchors are exactly the same is a fundamental part of being a safe climber. Chapter 6 covers the skills needed for evaluating, backing up, and lowering off of bolted anchors.

BELAY ANCHORS

On a multipitch route, the lead climber sets belay anchors at the end of each pitch and

Tommy Caldwell belaying high above a glacier in Patagonia, Argentina. This anchor bypasses the white rope left from an old fixed anchor; old nylon has unpredictable strength, so a smart climber avoids relying on such material.

belays her partner up. When the partner arrives at the belay station, they reorganize the rack and one of them leads above. When the leader starts up the next pitch, the belay anchors provide the climbing team's sole security (save the climbers' skills), and because there is little rope out to absorb the impact, a fall at this point can result in extremely high forces.

A good belay anchor generally has multiple anchors rigged together with cord or webbing to create a master point for clipping in. Chapter 7 shows how to rig belay anchors that are convenient, quick, clean—and bombproof. It also shows how to deal with some tricky anchoring situations and how to make do with minimal amounts of gear.

LEAD PROTECTION ANCHORS

Traditional, or "trad," climbers set their own protection anchors while leading to protect against a fall. The first climber leads a pitch, placing protection as she climbs. If she falls, she'll fall twice the distance to her last protection—providing that it holds. After she finishes the pitch and anchors herself, she belays the second climber, who removes the gear as he climbs. He has a top rope, so climbing second is safer and less psychologically demanding than leading. The second climber often leads the next pitch. Chapter 9 provides information on protecting a pitch when lead climbing.

Sport climbers protect sport routes by clipping preplaced anchor bolts. Chapter 6 discusses how to evaluate existing bolts, how to rig bolted belay anchors, and how to back up the bolts at a belay station. Many traditional climbs also use bolted anchors, so evaluation and understanding of these permanent anchors is important for all types of climbing.

BIG WALL ANCHORS

Aid climbers hang on most of the pieces they place, ascending terrain that lacks the hand- or footholds needed for free

Alex Honnold mixing it up with a combination of bolted and natural-protection anchors on steep rock in Germany

climbing, and as a result become highly tuned to the subtleties of anchoring. Hard aid climbers can spend hours ascending a single pitch, often setting a belay anchor that must withstand hauling, jugging, and the possibility of catching a gear-laden climber. Big-wall free climbing has similar anchor demands. This book does not cover specialized aid gear or techniques, but it does provide information that is useful for big-wall and aid climbing. Any aspiring trad climber will do well to take a day to learn how to aid climb simply because the process and constant reliance on the equipment is an ideal lesson on how to better use climbing gear.

FORCES ON CLIMBING ANCHORS

Aspire to always place anchors that, individually, would hold any fall or force that the climbing team could subject them to. This means that even a top-rope or rappel anchor, where the maximum force may be little more than body weight, should be set with the same care and approximate strength as an anchor for a hanging belay on a multipitch climb. However, perfect

CLEAN CLIMBING

When I began climbing in 1978, I learned much of my limited knowledge from Royal Robbins's Beginning Rockcraft *and* Advanced Rockcraft *books. When those books were created, some of the primary anchors used by climbers were pitons, which were beaten in and out of cracks with a hammer. The problem was, all of that pounding destroyed the rock. When chocks, and later cams, became available, most climbers embraced the new "clean climbing" ethic, using the new gear that could be placed and removed by hand without scarring the rock. But I didn't know that at the time.*

On my very first climb, I was leading and pounding pitons, until some climbers yelled up, "Hey! We don't use those pitons anymore!" After that I embraced clean climbing, too. Pitons are still useful for some alpine and aid climbs.

When a climber places a bolt, it becomes a permanent fixture in the rock. Bolts have enabled the creation of hundreds of thousands of great climbs (and more than a few trashy ones) around the world, but they definitely change the character of a cliff and an area. It is up to each climber to use good judgment and follow local tradition when placing pitons or bolts and to embrace clean climbing—by using removable anchors that do not require a hammer or drill—when the rock allows.

—Craig Luebben

placements are not always possible, so it is useful to understand how the forces vary depending on the scenario.

BODY WEIGHT

When top-roping, the climber is below the anchor, and the maximum load on the anchors will be the climber's weight and part of the belayer's weight; if the climber falls with slack in the rope, the force can be somewhat higher, but still well below the strength of solid anchors. If the rock is less than vertical, the force on the anchors decreases with the angle of the rock.

When rappelling, if the descent is smooth, the anchors hold only the climber's weight. A jerky rappel can drastically increase the force on the anchors, but solid rappel anchors will still easily withstand such a load.

The construction and rescue industries use safety factors for calculating the load that a structure must be capable of withstanding. For some applications, they use a safety factor of five—any structure or system must be five times stronger than any foreseeable load. In a laboratory setting, three solid anchors pre-equalized with a cordelette might hold more than 40 kN (about 9,000 pounds), giving an impressive safety factor of ten to twenty: the anchor is ten to twenty times stronger than needed for the body-weight loads created during top-roping or rappelling (and stronger than the carabiner you're clipped in with).

TOP ANCHORS

TOP-ROPING=
BODY-WEIGHT FORCES
ON ANCHOR

LEADING:
MANY TIMES MORE
FORCE ON ANCHOR

When considering the possible forces on anchors, it's essential to differentiate between body-weight situations and leader-fall forces—just because a piece will hold body weight doesn't mean it will hold a leader fall.

LEADER FALLS

When lead climbing, you can often toss this industrial safety factor out the window. Lead falls usually deliver all their force onto a single piece of protection, and the pulley effect (explained later in this chapter) can increase the impact force on the protection by 60 to 70 percent above the force of the falling climber. In the worst cases—when the climber is close to the belay and little rope is out—falls can come close to or exceed the strength of some climbing protection, especially tiny nuts, small cams, carabiners with the gates pushed open, sketchy fixed gear, poorly placed anchors, or anchors set in poor rock. Only bomber pieces can hold these worst-case falls, and even more reasonable climbing falls hammer the anchors with significant force.

The force in a vertical or overhanging leader fall is determined by the weight of the climber, the length of the fall, and by the rate of deceleration. The saving grace of high leader-fall forces is the dynamic rope, which stretches to dampen the climber's deceleration. In hard leader falls, a *dynamic belay*—in which some rope slips through the belay device and/or the belayer's body gets lifted—can also slow the falling climber and reduce the peak impact force. The rope slippage is not generally intentional; it is caused when the rope-pulling force on the brake hand exceeds the belayer's grip strength. Sometimes, a savvy belayer will allow some rope to slide through on purpose to soften a fall (gloves are essential here). Assisted-braking belay devices limit rope slippage and stop the fall *fast*; this increases the impact force but decreases the falling distance.

A load-limiting runner—one with stitches that blow out as the runner gets loaded—also slows the falling climber's deceleration rate and reduces the peak force. Once all the energy-absorbing stitches are blown, you have a full-strength runner that will allow the force to increase if the fall has not completely stopped. Ice climbers use load limiters because ice pro is often weaker than rock pro. Load limiters make the most difference on falls near the belay, where peak forces are high, but a good leader will almost always be able to find anchors that are plenty strong without using load limiters.

The force in a leader fall is roughly proportional to the climber's weight. Lighter climbers have a better chance that mediocre gear will catch a fall. Since the UIAA uses 80-kilogram (176-pound) test weights in its rope certification tests, heavier climbers might take extra precautions, like setting more protection, equalizing mediocre pieces, using load limiters on mediocre protection near the belay, and climbing on thicker ropes. But remember, smaller climbers taking meaty whippers generate far more force than bigger climbers taking short falls, so being of smaller stature doesn't mean sketchy gear will always hold your falls.

A leader needs to know when the forces may be high and place solid protection, back off, or climb with perfect control. Chapter 10 discusses climbing physics, forces on lead protection, and fall factors.

UNITS OF MEASURE

Most countries in the world have adopted the metric system, which uses newtons (N) and meters (m) to measure force and distance. In the United States, we are stuck using the imperial standard of pounds and feet from the British system, even though the Brits had the good sense to abandon it. Geology pays little attention to national boundaries, though, so climbers in the United States have adopted the metric system as the standard for climbing measurements. For example, the unit of force used to rate climbing gear is the kilonewton (kN), which is equal to 1,000 newtons or about 225 pounds of force. The metric system is so prevalent in climbing that even in the United States, the vast majority of climbing ropes and cords are sold in metric units; you can find a 10-millimeter rope in any climbing store, but ask around for a 3/8-inch climbing rope and you'll probably get some confused looks. In order to adhere to the international language of climbing, in this book we use metric units with imperial units shown in parentheses only when relevant. Thus, when referencing the dimensions for climbing gear that is universally sold and referred to in metric, such as rope or cord diameter, the imperial equivalent is not included. In cases where the hardware is borrowed from another industry and not manufactured specifically for climbing (such as bolt measurements of 10 millimeters or 3/8 inch), the metric measurement and the nearest manufactured imperial equivalent is provided.

High-force situations include the following:
- falling close to belay (high fall factor)
- long falling distance (high fall force)
- assisted-braking belay device (static belay)
- a heavy leader (high momentum)

HOW MANY ANCHORS?

When setting anchors for rappelling, top-roping, or building a belay station, two good bolts or three *bomber* pieces are standard protocol. When belaying a leader, an extra anchor is sometimes added to hold an upward pull.

Bomber means able to hold any climbing fall. Numerous climbers have reported, following an incident of a piece failing under a lead fall force, that the piece was "bomber." But if a piece failed, it was not bomber. If the pieces are not bomber, add more and/or equalize them. Likewise, if the pieces are small nuts and cams or cams in smooth downward-flaring placements (and by definition, not bomber), or if the rock quality is questionable, add more anchors. Having bomber anchors serves two purposes: it keeps you from hitting the deck if you fall *and* allows you to relax and enjoy climbing. Feel free to place extra gear just for peace of mind, but remember to save enough for the rest of the pitch.

As in so many areas of life, quality over quantity is the mantra: two bomber belay

The most important consideration for any anchor is to ask yourself, before you commit to it, "Do I trust this anchor with my life and my partner's?"

anchors are more reassuring than six shifty micronuts and microcams or any kind of gear in loose rock.

On a multipitch climb, the first piece of lead protection on each pitch protects the belay anchors from severe impact, and it makes a fall easier for the belayer to catch. The first piece is so critical that it can be considered part of the belay anchor, and in most cases it will likely receive a much greater force than the anchor itself. If the first protection isn't good, find better pro as soon as possible.

In alpine situations, or even rock climbing in adventurous places (or off-route), the climbing team sometimes relies on one or two pieces for an anchor. If the anchor is anything less than bomber, the leader should belay the second off her harness and bolster the anchors with her stance. If the climber falls, the belayer takes the weight on her braced body, with the anchors as a backup. This might be fine for belaying a second climber, but if the leader falls onto such a belay, the result can be disastrous. The body-belay

ERNEST

The problem with acronyms is that they encourage protocol rather than judgment-based decision-making. The climber who thinks, "If my anchor is ERNEST, I am set," is not as versatile or safe in difficult situations as the climber who analyzes the situation and crafts an appropriate, efficient solution. Still, acronyms are a useful mnemonic device for learning, and they can help you remember some key points.

When rigging multipoint anchors for a belay station, rappel station, or top rope, the acronym ERNEST sums up many important considerations:

E = Equalized. The load is distributed somewhat equally among the individual anchors so that the final rigged anchor achieves maximum strength.

R = Redundant. All components of the anchor are backed up, so any single failure does not result in a catastrophe.

NE = No Extension. If any anchor fails, extension in the rigging material is minimized to protect the remaining anchor(s) from receiving a higher impact load.

S = Solid. Each placement and the overall system, *including the rock,* must be solid enough for the situation.

T = Timely. Building the anchors is fast and efficient.

Remember, the acronym ERNEST does not convey priority; *solid* is, by far, the most important element.

strategy has little place in high-angle rock climbing, where good anchors are available and falling forces can be huge. You're usually better off downclimbing or continuing higher than belaying off a poor anchor.

Occasionally a belay, or more often a rappel, will be anchored off a large, well-rooted living tree. Trusting a single tree is a judgment call that must be made by the climbing team, but obviously a healthy, well-rooted tree with a large diameter is more than strong enough to serve as the sole climbing anchor. In some ecosystems, such as the isolated continent of Australia, root systems are much shallower than those of North American and European trees, so

if you're in a new region, talk to locals to learn how big a tree must be to trust it for a belay anchor.

HOW IMPORTANT IS EQUALIZATION?

By definition, equalization means distributing the load evenly among two or more pieces to increase the strength of the overall anchor. It's like putting all your team members on the rope in a tug-of-war. If you let two of them sit, ready to work only when disaster is imminent, you'll never achieve the team's maximum pulling strength. Likewise in an anchor: if all of the pieces are not sharing the load, the anchor is weaker than it could be.

Often you don't need all the tug-of-war team members pulling, though. When top-roping or rappelling, it's like having grade school kids pulling against NFL linemen. Two-thirds of the linemen can sit down, and you still have no contest. The same with the anchors: if you have three bomber cams, each capable of holding 14 kN (3,150 pounds), then any of the pieces can easily hold the 2–4 kN (450–900 pounds) of force in average free-climbing falls, with the rest serving as a backup, so equalization isn't as crucial. These are the kinds of belay anchors you want.

When the leader is climbing directly above the belay with no protection, your anchors are up against the NFL linemen. You want them all working to produce maximum strength, so it's smart to equalize. And the same goes for mediocre or bad belay anchors or lead protection—setting more pieces and equalizing them is stronger.

For maximum strength, you would actually want to spread the load proportionately to the strength of each individual piece—stronger pieces would hold more force and weaker pieces would hold less. But no one can predict the exact strength of each piece or distribute precise fractions of the load to each piece. Instead, when it's important to equalize, we strive for equal load distribution among the pieces: theoretically, a two-piece anchor gets a fifty-fifty split, three pieces hold one-third each, and a four-piece anchor spreads one-quarter of the load to each piece.

In reality, the knots, lengths of cord, friction over edges, and precise angle of pull all make an equal division of force unlikely, but it's possible to get close.

Some rigging systems equalize better than others, so it comes back to judgment-based decision-making: you have to determine what kind of force might hit the anchor, how strong the individual pieces are, what type of anchor rigging is most convenient and strong enough for the job, and how much time you want to spend building the anchor. In climbing, it often pays to be conservative; if in doubt, equalize.

PRE-EQUALIZED ANCHORS

Pre-equalized rigging creates a convenient "work station" at the anchor, and it's a relatively fast, simple way to build anchors that are redundant and allow no extension if an anchor blows. A pre-equalized anchor consists of a cordelette or double-length sling extending to each piece and tied off to create a master point that connects the climbers to all of the anchors. The single clipping point is especially convenient when one climber leads many pitches in a row, or when the team has more than two climbers.

The downside to pre-equalizing? First, it takes time, and when the protection is perfect, pre-equalization is not necessary. While alternating leads with bomber anchors on a long climb, pre-equalizing every anchor eats up both time and gear. An efficient climber will learn to rig bomber, near-equalized anchors without using a cordelette.

Pre-equalizing a double sling (one that fits nicely over the shoulder when doubled) is one of the simplest ways to create a redundant, somewhat equalized two-point anchor.

A. Clip the slings into both bolts.

B. Pull two loops down between the bolts toward the anticipated direction of loading. Keep the stitching up close to one of the bolts so it is out of the way of your knot in the next step.

C. Tie an overhand knot or figure eight in the sling to create a "master point" (sometimes called the power point) while keeping the sling oriented toward the anticipated direction of pull. The figure-eight knot uses more sling than an overhand but is easier to untie after weighting.

D. Tie your lead rope in to a locking carabiner clipped to the master point.

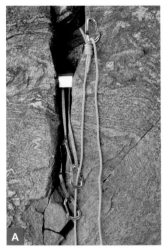

A cordelette is a 5- to 6.5-meter (16- to 22-foot) length of 5.5- or 6-millimeter-diameter Spectra (Dyneema in Europe), or 7-millimeter-diameter perlon. Use it to conveniently rig three- or four-point anchors to ERNEST standards.

A. Tie the cordelette into a loop with a double fisherman's or other suitable knot (most guides use a flat overhand). Clip the cordelette in to all the anchors.

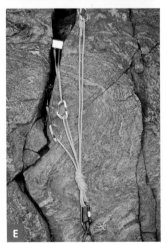

B. Pull down a length of cord between each anchor in the expected direction of loading or pull.

C. Tie a figure-eight knot in the cordelette (or an overhand if you don't have enough cord for a figure eight) while keeping the strands running to each piece tight in the anticipated direction of pull.

D. This creates two places to clip in and belay: the master point at the bottom of the loop and the "top shelf" by clipping through each loop created by the strands running to each anchor.

E. Clipping in to the master point connects you to all the anchors.

Second, pre-equalizing doesn't always distribute the load equally between the pieces. If the loading direction varies, all of the force can descend onto one piece. A single piece can also take the brunt of the force if it's connected to a short leg in the cordelette because that leg will stretch the least. If the anchors are spread vertically, the leg lengths will be unequal and so will the load distribution.

If the anchors are spread horizontally, with the leg lengths roughly equal and adjusted well for the direction of pull, a pre-equalized sling or cordelette can spread the load fairly well and does increase the overall strength of the anchor. In one series of tests conducted by Craig Luebben at the Sterling Rope testing lab, three-point anchors that were spread horizontally and rigged with a cordelette consistently held above 40 kN (about 9,000 pounds).

With bomber pieces, it's hard to create a load that makes them fail no matter how you rig them. Even if all the stars were to align against you to create a worst-case fall onto a belay anchor that was not equalized, most of the fall's momentum would be gone by the time a solid piece failed, and the other bomber pieces would easily handle the remaining load.

If the pieces aren't bomber, you can create enough force in a fall to rip them out. In this case, or if the loading direction on the anchors might change, rigging with the sliding X or the equalizer (see next section) will distribute the load better and give more strength than a pre-equalized setup;

but you should strive to never belay off an anchor built with dubious placements.

Many guides tie their cordelette into a loop with a flat overhand knot because it's quick to tie and easy to adjust (see appendix 2). Always cinch the knot tight and leave tails at least 30 centimeters (1 foot) long. A double fisherman's knot (or triple fisherman's, if the cord manufacturer recommends it) is a little stronger; use one of these knots in instances when you expect a high load on the cord, such as if you're using a single loop of cordelette for lead protection.

SELF-EQUALIZING ANCHORS

The idea behind self-equalizing is to split the force equally between the pieces, with the ability to adjust to different directions of pull while weighted. The sliding X is one of the few ways to achieve this nearly perfect equalization between multiple pieces. The sliding X is quick and convenient and spreads the load fairly evenly among the pieces.

The equalizer splits the load even more precisely because you don't have the friction of the sliding X running through the carabiner; however, removing the knots after heavily weighting the anchor is not easy. When each individual piece of an anchor is bomber, it is more efficient to use the cordelette or other rigging methods that are easier to disassemble.

Any self-equalizing system extends somewhat if one piece of the anchor fails. If you allow too much extension in the rigging and an anchor blows, the fall gets longer.

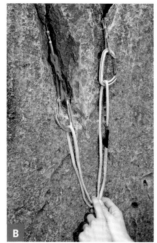

A self-equalizing arrangement allows the clipping carabiner to slide toward the direction of pull, even if this direction changes, and divide the load evenly between the anchors. If the anchors are equalized with a shoulder-length sling (one that fits nicely when placed over the shoulder), the extension will not be large if one anchor fails. These photos show an equalized anchor clipped on lead, not at a belay anchor.

A. Clip the sling in to both anchors.
B. Pull two strands of sling down between the anchors.
C. Put a 180-degree twist in one of the strands.
D. Clip in to both loops to equalize the load.

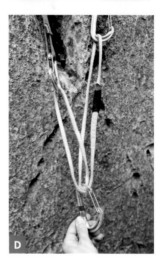

Left: If there is no twist in the sling and one piece fails, the carabiner will slide off the end of the sling and webbing, dropping the climber.

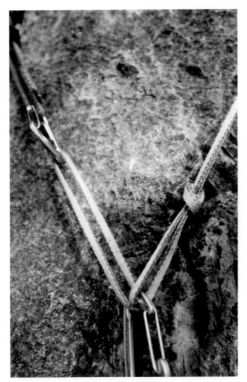

If one leg of the sliding X is long, you can add an extension-limiting knot to the longer leg. This is particularly important if the anchor attached to the long leg is less than bomber, because if it fails, there will be a significant drop before the second anchor is weighted. The knot will minimize the extension.

If both legs of the sling are long, add two extension-limiting knots to minimize extension in case either anchor fails. With two limiting knots, the sliding X becomes a redundant clipping point. Adjust the knots up or down the webbing to allow for change in the direction of pull, without allowing too much extension if one anchor fails.

This can create extra impact force on the remaining anchors, and the moving anchor point could force the belayer to lose control of the rope. You can limit the extension to a few inches by tying extension-limiting knots in the longer legs of the webbing or cord.

Beware of situations where the sliding X, or any anchor-rigging method, pulls the individual pieces into a weaker orientation, such as pulling a chock slightly upward or a cam onto a downward-flaring surface.

Create a sliding X with more than two pieces.

A. *You can equalize the load on three or even four pieces with the sliding* X. *Extend the anchors as necessary to bring the clipping points close together (here, the middle piece has been extended with a sling). Two slings are used for redundancy. Treat the slings as one.*

B. *Pull two loops down between the pieces.*

C. *Twist an* X *into both loops.*

D. *Clip all three loops to equalize the load between the three pieces. Use a large carabiner so the webbing can easily slide to adjust. If one anchor fails, the slack from that loop is split between the other two loops, so extension is minimal.*

E. *Clipping two or more climbers plus a belay device in to all the loops of the sliding* X *can be tricky. A nice solution is to designate a large locked carabiner as "master carabiner" to function as the master point. Then everyone clips in and out of the master carabiner.*

Using a factory-made equalizer.
A. The equalizer makes it easy to equalize the load on a three-point anchor. Simply clip the ends in to the outside pieces and a bight in to the center piece.
B. Tie a figure eight in the resulting loop and clip it. The knot minimizes extension if a piece fails and creates redundancy in the webbing of the equalizer.

V-ANGLE

The V-angle is the angle formed by the legs of the sling or cord. The larger the V-angle, the harder each anchor must pull against the other to hold the downward force. At 60 degrees, the force on both anchors is 15 percent greater than the pulling force; at 90 degrees, it's 41 percent greater. When you reach 120 degrees, the force doubles, and it triples at 141 degrees. At 175 degrees the load multiplies more than twentyfold. For building anchors, a V-angle up to 60 degrees keeps the force reasonable, and an angle of 90 degrees is probably okay for solid anchors.

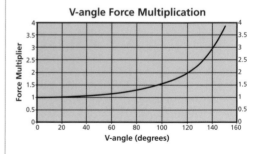

V-ANGLE Graph A.
As the angle formed by the sling or cord increases above 0 degrees, the force on the anchors increases. The increase is moderate at smaller angles.

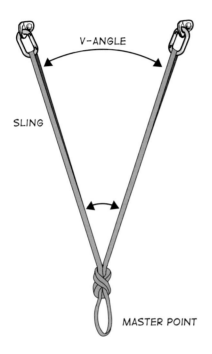

The V-angle is the angle between the legs of the sling or cord attached to the anchors.

V-angle Force Multiplication

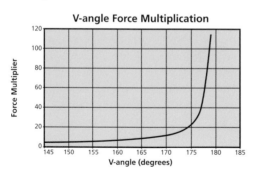

V-ANGLE Graph B.
As the angle approaches 180 degrees, the force increases exponentially.

This relatively shallow V-angle of 55 degrees causes a small increase in the load on the anchors, which will now be about 13 percent greater than the pulling force. (Note: this image shows an equalized anchor on lead, with only a single nonlocking carabiner—a belay would use a locking or two nonlocking carabiners.)

This wide V-angle of about 100 degrees increases the force on the anchors by nearly 60 percent.

FORCE = $1^2/_3$

FORCE = 1

FORCE = $^2/_3$

The pulley effect. The top protection gets loaded by both the falling climber and the belayer, increasing the total load by 60–70 percent in addition to the force of the falling climber.

PULLEY EFFECT

In a leader fall, the top protection must hold the sum of the forces on the climber and the belayer. This is called the *pulley effect*. Friction at the top anchor causes the force on the belayer to be only about two-thirds of the force on the leader, depending on the rope and the carabiner's rope-bearing surface, and assuming that the rope is running clean, with little rope drag. This nearly doubles the impact force on the top anchor beyond the force of the falling climber.

The pulley effect does have a good side: it allows us to create a mechanical advantage in hauling systems.

MULTIDIRECTIONAL ANCHORS

On a multipitch climb, it's beneficial to have a multidirectional belay anchor (one that can handle a pull in any direction) so that a hard leader fall does not lift the belayer *and* the anchors from their perch. If the pitch traverses at the beginning or end, the anchors should also be able to handle a sideways pull.

The first piece of protection in a pitch should be able to handle pulls in the downward or outward direction; otherwise a fall might pop out the first piece, then the second, and so on up the rope. Any lead protection where the rope changes direction should be able to hold both a downward pull and a sideways pull; otherwise, that piece may fail during a lead fall.

OPPOSING NUTS

Wired nuts can oppose each other to create a multidirectional anchor in a horizontal, vertical, or even diagonal crack. One standard way to oppose two nuts is to tie them together on a sling with clove hitches and cinch the clove hitches tight. This method doesn't create active tension, so the nuts don't lock each other in the crack very well. The cinch method shown here creates live tension to hold the nuts in place. You can also set chocks or cams in opposition or rig a sketchy fixed piton to oppose a good wired nut so the nut doesn't get tugged out of the crack by the rope.

A. Set two opposing nuts about 60–100 centimeters (2–3 feet) apart. Clip a sling in to one of the nuts and pass both strands of the sling through a carabiner attached to the other nut.
B. Pass the end of the sling between its own two strands and again through the carabiner attached to the second nut.
C. Cinch the sling tight to create tension between the two nuts.
D. Clip the sling.

Bolts, fixed pitons, trees, threads, and well-placed Big Bros are all multidirectional. To some degree, cams set in a parallel placement are multidirectional because they can swivel to adjust to new loading directions.

Because of the large V-angle between the horizontally spaced nuts and the resulting force multiplication, be careful trusting this arrangement to catch a hard leader fall. In a vertical crack, you don't get the large V-angle, though you get some extra force on the upper piece due to the pulley effect: the upper carabiner must hold both the falling climber and the pull from the lower anchor. This effect is diminished by the friction in the sling where it wraps through the carabiner, so the pulley effect should be modest.

CLIMBER ATTACHMENT TO THE ANCHORS

Whenever you're at an exposed belay or rappel station, you clip yourself to the anchors. Depending on the situation, you

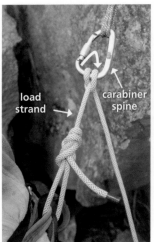

Most guides tie in with a clove hitch because it's easy to adjust, and once you unclip the knot, it's gone—nothing left to untie. When belaying a leader, it's wise to set the load strand—the rope strand running to the belayer—close to the carabiner spine (not the gate) to get maximum strength from the carabiner.

The ultra-secure figure eight on a bight makes a good choice for clipping in to the anchors.

If a locking carabiner isn't available, substitute two standard carabiners. Orient the gates so that they open in opposite directions and set them both with gates opening down. That way, if one carabiner flips around, one gate opens up while the other opens down to prevent accidental unclipping.

can tie in with the climbing rope or girth-hitch a sling or daisy chain to your harness and clip it to the anchor master point. Clipping with a locking carabiner is best, but you can also substitute two standard carabiners with the gates opposed and reversed. Generally you want to be attached tight to the anchors, without slack in your rope or sling.

ROPE

If the team is climbing a multipitch route, clip the rope directly to the anchor master point with a locking carabiner for the most secure and convenient attachment. If swapping leads, the second person is only stopping at the belay briefly to rerack, so they can simply stay on belay and clip to anchors with a sling or daisy chain rather than tying in with the rope.

SLING

During rappels, the rope is free from the climbing team, so each member needs another method for attaching to the

A sewn sling can be girth-hitched to the harness belay loop or tie-in points and clipped to the anchor master point. This is a good way to attach to the anchors on a multi-rappel descent. Do not use the girth hitch if you expect heavy shock loading, such as a factor-2 fall.

Two slings girth-hitched to the harness provide redundancy. Girth-hitch them simultaneously (treat two slings as one) to save a step in the setup. You can clip each of the slings to a different anchor point as shown or clip both slings to the anchor master point (usually with a single locking carabiner).

A double-length sling clipped in to the anchor gives more extension. You can adjust the effective length of the double sling by tying an overhand knot at the exact length you desire.

41

anchors. A single- or double-length shoulder sling girth-hitched to the harness belay loop or tie-in points makes a convenient loop for clipping the anchors.

DAISY CHAIN

Daisy chains are almost indispensable for aid climbing on big walls, and many climbers use them for cragging and multi-pitch free climbing. Some climbers prefer the simplicity of anchoring with the rope or slings, while others find the convenience of the daisy useful. Sometimes it depends on the rope system the team is using.

The daisy or sling should not be the sole attachment to the anchors when belaying a leader; the rope should also be connected to the anchors for its sheer strength and dynamic qualities.

girth hitch

harness belay loop

The daisy chain has many loops so that you can easily adjust your extension from the anchors. Most daisy chains load a single bar-tack of stitching at a time, so a high load can begin blowing out the daisy loops.

DANGER

The dangerous daisy. Never clip more than one daisy loop into a single carabiner; breaking a few loops can cause the daisy to completely unclip from the anchors. This is critically dangerous if two adjacent or nearby loops are clipped in to the same carabiner, as shown here. Break a few bar-tacks, and you're gone.

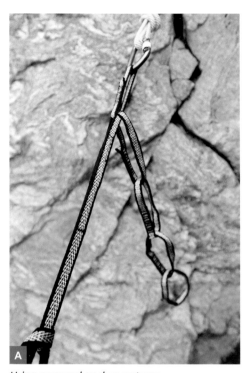

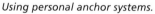

Using personal anchor systems.

A. *A personal anchor system (PAS) is a chain of full-strength loops that provides several attachment lengths. The bomber loops alleviate the problem of bar-tack blowouts that are possible with a daisy chain. Here, the PAS attaches the climber to the anchor master point.*

B. *A PAS (or daisy chain) can also be used to clip in to two bolts. This system doesn't provide any equalization, so it's only good if the bolts are bomber and if the leader isn't likely to fall onto the belay anchors. The hitch is the weak point in this system.*

BAD: Watch your gates! Keep the carabiners oriented so the gates are closed. An open carabiner has only 30–45 percent of the strength of a closed one.

BELAYING THE SECOND

Several techniques exist for belaying the second. The "best" technique depends on the situation, the climbing team's preferences, and the quality of the anchors. The rope system or belay techniques of the team may influence the way they arrange the belay anchors.

climber top strand

to climber

The "guide's belay." It's a cinch to belay directly off the anchors with an autoblocking belay device, because the belay device automatically locks the rope if the climber falls or hangs. The rope diameter must meet the device manufacturer's specifications, and the device must be rigged correctly or it will not lock in a fall.

Guides often clip themselves in to the top shelf of the cordelette (the loops coming from each anchor, just above the cordelette's figure-eight knot) to keep the master point uncluttered for their partners. Clipping each individual loop connects you to all the anchors. When using the top shelf, first cinch the figure eight tight. If the master point loop is short, put a carabiner in the master point so the knot cannot roll.

DIRECT BELAY

A direct belay with an autoblocking belay device keeps the belayer out of the system. The weight of a falling or hanging climber goes straight onto the anchors, so it's effortless to hold a climber. The direct belay also makes it easy to haul your partner, as shown in chapter 5, and to escape the belay in an emergency.

The direct belay works for belaying only the climber(s) following a pitch; it doesn't work for belaying a leader. There are more than a dozen autoblocking belay devices currently on the market. Make sure you understand the manufacturer's instructions before using one of these devices; they all require specific rigging for autoblocking, plus additional techniques for lowering a hanging climber.

Belaying directly off the anchors with an assisted-braking device can work great. Make sure the moving parts of the device don't press against anything when the device is loaded or it may not engage. The belayer is clipped in to the master point here.

For a quick, improvised belay, rig a Munter hitch right off the anchors. This works okay for short belays or lowers, but the Munter kinks a long length of rope.

Belaying directly off the anchors with a standard belay device can be awkward or even dangerous. You need to keep the rope bent across the device to ensure adequate friction in a fall.

REDIRECTED BELAY

If the climber falls or hangs, a redirected belay creates the pulley effect on the anchors: some of the belayer's weight comes onto the anchors to counter the weight of the climber. This increases the load on the anchors, so avoid the redirected belay if the anchors are not bomber.

The redirected belay is used by many climbers, because it's easy to hold a hanging climber and it works with a standard belay device attached directly to the harness. If the climber significantly outweighs the belayer, the belayer should be anchored against an upward pull, or a fall may lift her into the anchors.

(If the anchors are not great, though, the first choice is to search for better anchors.) In a hanging belay, the belayer's weight is already on the anchors, so redirecting the belay does not increase the force on the anchors.

BELAY OFF THE HARNESS

Belaying the second climber off your harness works well if your partner is climbing fast and isn't likely to fall. Belaying off the

When belaying off the harness, the belayer should be well positioned for catching a fall. The letters ABC describe the lineup: anchors, belayer, climber. The belayer should be in line between the anchors and the climber to keep from getting pulled off his stance while trying to hold a fall.

DANGER

The belayer is not in line between the anchors and the climber, and she has extra slack in her tie-in. If the climber falls, she'll get pulled off her stance and possibly lose control of the rope.

If the belay anchors aren't great, keep looking. If no other options exist, beef them up with a braced leg and good stance. The more parallel your braced leg is to the rope, the better you'll be able to hold a pull. The braced-leg anchor is not good for belaying the leader; a short leader fall by a small climber will generate far more force than even a big, strong belayer can withstand.

harness traps you into the system, though, making it uncomfortable to hold a hanging climber and difficult to escape the belay in an emergency. For this reason, many climbers prefer using an autoblocking belay device directly on the anchors.

BELAYING THE LEADER

When belaying a leader, you'll belay directly off your harness, preferably with the belay device connected to the harness belay loop.

UPWARD ANCHOR FOR BELAYING

Before belaying a leader, consider whether an upward-pull anchor is important. Belayers often do not anchor themselves when belaying from flat ground.

Another option in this scenario is to use the Edelrid Ohm on the belay or the first piece to reduce the force on the belayer. See chapter 8, Gym Anchors, for instruction on using the Ohm.

upward-pull
anchor

Above: *An upward-pull anchor can be clipped directly to the belay loop so any force goes right onto the anchor. This will provide a fairly static belay but can be useful for small climbers belaying large climbers.*

upward-pull
anchor

upward-pull
anchor

Above: *You can use the rope to connect to an upward-pull anchor. Clove-hitch the master point, cinch it tight, and then clove-hitch the upward anchor and cinch the clove hitches tight against each other. The rigging will allow some belayer lift, but not much.*

Left: *You can connect the upward anchor to the back of your harness using a girth-hitched sling, as shown here. You can also clip the anchor to your haul loop, provided it is full strength.*

   An upward-pull ground anchor may be warranted when top-roping if the climber seriously outweighs the belayer or if the belayer is likely to get pulled sideways. Don't use this method where rockfall is possible.

An upward anchor is warranted if

- the climber is considerably larger than the belayer, or
- the belay is away from the wall, so a fall could slam the belayer into the wall.

An upward-pull anchor will keep you from getting lifted if the leader takes a whipper. Remember, though, once you're anchored you are a sitting duck for falling rocks; do it in a safe area.

When belaying on a multipitch climb, anchors are mandatory (except—possibly—on the first pitch). Most of the anchors are set for a downward pull, with the belayer positioned below the anchors. A hard fall can still lift the belayer, unless a specific upward anchor is set to prevent this. It's often good for the belayer to lift a bit in a fall because it gives a more dynamic belay, decreasing the force on the climber and the top anchor. However, it's not good for the belayer to get lifted if she smashes into a roof or another rock feature, so use a direct upward-pull anchor when dangerous features exist.

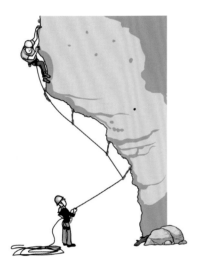 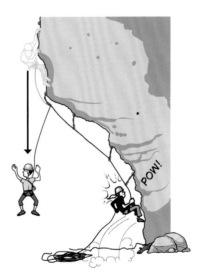

Do not belay a leader while standing far away from the wall or far to the side of the first protection piece unless you're anchored. Otherwise, if the leader falls, he might drag you into the wall, causing him to fall farther and possibly causing you to lose control of the belay rope. Even if you are anchored, belaying far off to the side puts extra slack in the lead rope, causing the leader to fall farther than necessary if he comes off. In cases where the belayer dramatically outweighs the climber, the belayer can intentionally stand a few feet to the side or out from a multidirectional first piece, such as a bolt; the resulting angle in the rope will work to cushion the leader as the belayer's body is pulled a bit horizontally with the force of the fall.

A recent development in our understanding of climbing physics involves the extreme forces in a factor-2 fall (a fall two times the length of rope out, such as a leader fall directly onto the belay) or even a hard fall onto the first piece or two while the leader is close to the belay. The forces generated in these cases are so high that it is quite possible to injure the belayer or cause them to drop the belay rope. For this reason, if hard climbing near the belay is expected or a runout is anticipated directly above the belay, consider belaying with a Munter hitch attached directly to the anchor for the first part of the pitch (A).

The anchor must be a perfect multidirectional anchor. The belayer should feed 9 or 12 meters (30 or 40 feet) of rope through the belay device (B) and tie a backup knot below the device (C). When the leader gets to a stance a few pieces above the belay, the belayer can switch back to a regular belay off her harness.

SHOCK LOADING

Many climbers and climbing instructors misuse the term *shock loading* to describe the extra-high impact that develops if, as a result of anchor failure, you get extension in the anchor rigging. While you do want to avoid excessive extension in your rigging, a little extension will lead to the fall being only slightly longer, thus increasing the force a little bit. There is no truly super-elevated shock load when you have a dynamic lead rope in the system.

ROCK TYPE AND QUALITY

Good rock quality is critical for setting strong climbing anchors—no anchor can be stronger than the rock it's set in. The strength of the rock depends on the rock type and the condition of the rock surrounding the anchor. Is it solid, fractured, or rotten? An experienced climber automatically assesses rock quality before setting an anchor (or pulling on a hold). Large blocks and flakes can be particularly misleading—big does not necessarily mean solid. If you set an anchor behind a loose flake or block, you could pull the rock off with you in a fall.

Many different rock types exist in the thousands of climbing areas in the world. Granite (and granitelike variations), sandstone, and limestone are the three most prevalent rock types for climbing. Good solid granite provides an excellent medium for rock anchors because the rock is usually strong and solid. Even in good granite, though, you need to beware of rotten or fractured areas. Places like Yosemite, where the granite is impeccably solid most of the time, has loose flakes, teetering blocks, and rotten rock that can surprise the unwary climber.

Sandstone varies in quality from super hard and strong to so soft that it disintegrates like sugar when touched. Fortunately, looking at and touching the rock (and sometimes hitting, kicking, or tapping it with a cam or nut) will provide an assessment of how solid the rock is. Some sandstone has a patina of mineral-hardened rock on the surface, such as the Wingate Sandstone in Indian Creek, Utah, and the Aztec Sandstone in Red Rocks, Nevada. This patina makes the rock surface harder and stronger, but it can mask underlying soft rock. When a cam gets heavily loaded in this type of rock, the cam lobes can punch through the patina into the softer rock and then slide out of the crack, leaving a set of "cam tracks" on each side of the crack. For this reason, it's wise to place protection frequently in soft sandstone.

Limestone is fun to climb because it's so featured, but it generally doesn't fracture cleanly like granite or sandstone. This can make it difficult to set removable anchors, which explains why most limestone climbing areas are bolted. When you do set protection anchors in limestone, the crack surfaces are often convoluted, so take care that the anchor sits well in the crack. Sometimes the best option is to set protection in the pockets that are prevalent in limestone.

Dozens of other rock types create a good medium for climbing. It's wise to judge the rock quality for climbing and anchoring before committing to a route and to continually reassess as you climb. Speaking with locals about rock quality is another way to add invaluable information to your assessment and decision-making.

EXERCISE—BUILDING ANCHOR STATIONS

Set three anchors relatively close together. Practice rigging the following arrangements:

- pre-equalized two-piece anchor with a double sling
- pre-equalized three-piece anchor with a cordelette
- sliding X with a shoulder-length sling
- sliding X with two extension-limiting knots
- three-loop sliding X
- equalizer
- opposing nuts
- direct belay with an assisted-braking belay device
- redirected belay
- belay off harness with a rope tie-in

Opposite: *Berndt Arnold hard climbing above a natural thread, Elbsandstein, Germany*

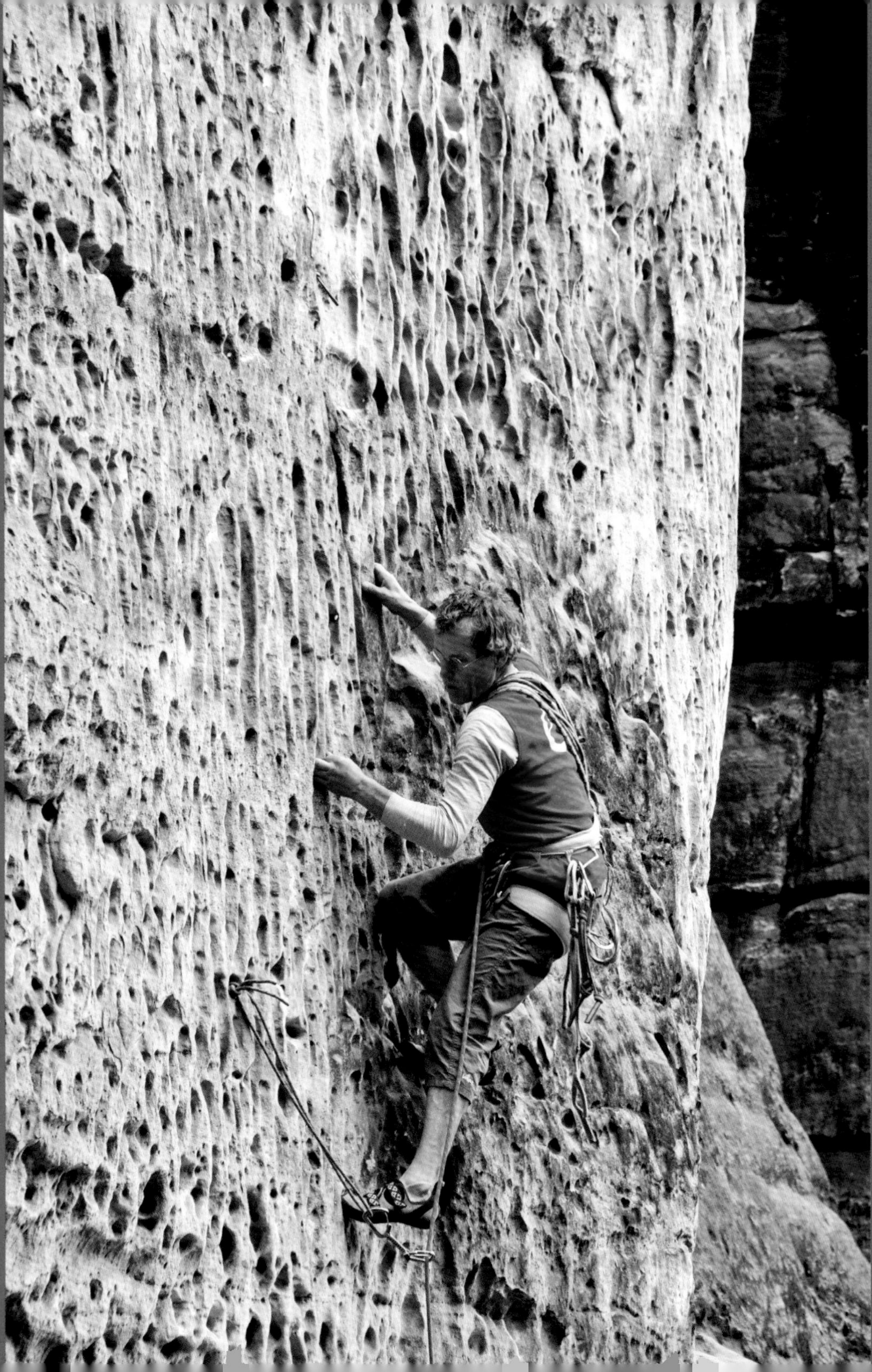

CHAPTER 2

Natural and Fixed Anchors

Let's say you're climbing a route like the classic *Yellow Spur* in Colorado's Eldorado Canyon. You carry a slim rack because the pitches are short and loads of fixed gear exist. You take the easier start and climb with unwavering control to the first piton, 15 feet up, which is adorned with a loop of ratty nylon webbing. You clip the piton directly with a shoulder-length sling rather than placing any faith in the faded sling. You continue smooth and steady, still unwilling to fall because you don't really trust the old rusted piton. As soon as you can set a good cam, you relax. You avoid clipping another piton because it is off to the side and would cause rope drag; instead you set another good cam, which you trust more anyway. At the end of the pitch, you anchor to a decent-sized tree draped with nylon slings from retreating climbers, and call, "Off belay!"

The next two pitches offer some natural protection, which you bypass because the rock looks loose. You do thread a rock tunnel above some of the bad rock, though. On the *Yellow Spur*'s famous crux arête pitch, you leave the exposed belay and clip a series of old fixed pitons. None of them looks great, but there are so many pins, all close together, that you feel safe. Higher up, you clip a modern 10-millimeter-diameter (³⁄₈-inch) bolt, and you know you have good protection. The next piece, however, is a rusty 6-millimeter (¼-inch) bolt left from some decades ago. You sure don't trust that one; in fact, you don't even clip it. Instead you climb a little higher to another good bolt, and finally an old bent piton that protects the crux moves. You clip the pin but don't trust it much, and you are happy to have that solid bolt not far below. On the final pitch, you wrap the top of the arête with a long sling to protect the second climber and then traverse to the route's exit.

As on the *Yellow Spur*, many traditional routes have a combination of natural, fixed, and climber-set anchors for protection and belay anchors. It's actually fun being

RESPECT THE TREES AND PLANTS

We climbers have a duty to respect and protect our natural environment. Heavy climbing traffic around trees can erode the soil or damage a tree's roots and bark. This can ultimately kill the tree and surrounding plants. In many situations, it's better to avoid using trees for anchors if other options exist. Trees rooted in shallow soil are especially vulnerable (and maybe not safe anyway). In some areas, fixed anchors have been installed to protect trees from climber traffic.

If you must rappel from a tree, leave a sling rather than feeding the rope directly around the tree. That way, to retrieve the rope, you pull it through the sling, or better, the rappel rings or carabiners attached to the sling, rather than across the bark.

In at least one case, crampon damage from ice climbers destroyed the roots and/or soil holding a tree in place. When two climbers used the tree as a rappel anchor, as had many climbers before, the tree came free; the tree and both climbers plummeted to the ground.

creative and using many different types of anchors to protect your climb.

This chapter discusses natural and fixed anchors, including

- trees,
- boulders,
- blocks,
- flakes,
- chockstones,
- horns and spikes,
- threads,
- pitons,
- bolts.

Natural anchors are often quick and easy to rig, and they require only a sling or cord and a carabiner, saving your chocks and cams for other placements. A climber needs to use common sense about what's strong enough—a tied-off branch or loose flake doesn't make a strong anchor, but an obviously solid feature can make a bomber anchor. This chapter will discuss the different types of natural anchors, how to evaluate them, and how to sling them.

The fixed hardware found on many cliffs runs the gamut from perfectly solid to unpredictable to obviously bad. Fortunately, motivated climbers have made a push in recent years to replace most of the old bolts and many of the fixed pitons, but plenty of sketchy fixed gear still exists. We'll discuss how to evaluate pitons and how to discriminate between good modern bolts and old untrustworthy bolts. The end of the chapter also includes a short discussion about fixed chocks and cams left behind after they got stuck in a crack.

NATURAL ANCHORS

Many natural anchors, including trees, threads, and some well-wedged chockstones, are multidirectional. Boulders, blocks, and flakes can also be multidirectional, depending on how they are slung. Slung horns or spikes, on the other hand, will usually hold only a downward pull.

TREES

Trees are easy to sling, provided you don't have to crawl through gnarly branches to reach the trunk. Before trusting a tree for anchoring, make sure

- the roots reach deep into cracks in the rock or into a large, deep patch of soil;
- the tree has living leaves or conifer needles;
- the tree diameter is large enough to inspire confidence.

There is no definitive guideline for safe tree diameter because different types of trees have different strengths, and the root structure strongly influences a tree's strength. However, any reasonably large tree that can withstand the high wind loads common in many climbing areas should be very strong.

Climbers often use a single large tree as their sole belay or rappel anchor. The climbing team must make a wise judgment call before placing total faith in the tree. A single tree does not provide redundant anchor, so make sure it's a strong one and consider doubling the cord or sling around the tree.

To make the sling redundant, pass it around the tree and tie it off with a figure-eight or overhand knot. This creates two independent wraps of webbing for redundancy.

If the tree is too large to tie off with the available material, you can simply girth-hitch it. Set the sling so that the clipping loop runs almost straight through the opposite loop in the webbing. Ideally, use two slings to make the webbing redundant.

If you must use smaller trees for an anchor, use two or more and equalize the load. Set the webbing near the ground to minimize leverage on the trees.

Often you have many smaller trees growing close together; in this case you can tie off the whole lot of them.

Danger! This anchor has three big problems: the tree is small and not very strong; the sling should be set near the ground to minimize leverage on this small tree; and the girth hitch bends back across itself, which drastically increases the stress on the webbing.

BOULDERS AND BLOCKS

Large boulders, blocks, and flakes can make great natural anchors—if they're solid. Sometimes it's difficult to judge the stability of a block or flake. Before trusting the rock feature, look at the contact surfaces where it meets the rock wall or the ledge. If the surface beneath a boulder or block slopes downward, if the boulder or block rests on debris, or if the boulder is round, it may not be stable. A very large boulder or block that sits flat on a ledge should be pretty strong.

This boulder has been tied off with a cordelette using two independent wraps for redundancy. Be extremely careful when using boulders for anchors—even a large boulder can be just a tug away from tipping over or sliding.

FLAKES

Flakes, even small ones, can make good anchors if they are solidly connected to the wall. Before using a flake as an anchor (or even as a hand- or foothold), inspect it for cracks. If the bottom of the flake is solidly connected to the wall, it may make a good anchor; if the flake's bottom has any cracks, though, don't trust it. A flake that's not well attached can be hazardous. If you use the flake for protection and fall, you might pull the whole thing off; now you are falling *and* the flake is falling behind you.

A flake can be a good anchor if it is solidly attached to the wall, the sling wraps securely over the flake, and the lead rope does not lift the sling off the flake.

When slinging all but the largest flakes, set the webbing or cord near the flake's bottom to minimize leverage on the flake. Be careful that the sling material does not contact sharp edges on the flake. If so, move the sling or add an extra sling for redundancy.

HORNS AND SPIKES

A sling around a solid horn or spike of rock makes a quick, easy anchor—but only for a downward pull. The rock needs to be solid and needs to have a positive lip to hold the sling in place.

If a horn is used for lead protection, you might tie a slipknot to help hold it in place. This works especially well on chicken heads, which have a bigger diameter at the head of the horn than at the throat (like a chicken's head).

CHOCKSTONES

A chockstone is a rock that either has fallen and become wedged into a crack over time or has been placed intentionally—to back up dubious rappel anchors or in other dire situations. A chockstone can make a good anchor if it's wedged securely and if the chockstone and rock walls are solid. Be cautious of huge sketchy chockstones that could fall or roll and hurt you. Before trusting a chockstone, *carefully* test its stability. It's often best to girth-hitch a sling on the edge of the chockstone where it meets the rock wall so that the potential force on the sling does not roll the chockstone.

DANGER

This chockstone is slung correctly.

This chockstone is not slung correctly; the sling is set in a way that may cause the chockstone to roll.

CHOKES AND THREADS

A solid thread will hold a pull in any direction. Estimate the strength of the thread based on the thickness and quality of the rock that supports the sling or cord. Be careful with sharp edges where the sling or cord contacts the rock. If the fit is tight, it can be tricky to feed the sling—a nut tool might help.

You can wrap a sling through a spot where two boulders or other rock features come together.

A thread and choke used for lead protection in Germany's Elbsandstein, where metal protection is not allowed.

Sometimes you can thread a natural tunnel in the rock with a sling or piece of cord to create an anchor—in this case two small threads are used together.

FIXED ANCHORS

Bolts, and sometimes pitons, are fixed in place for all climbers to use until they rust away or get replaced with new hardware. Occasionally you also find nuts and cams stuck in the crack. Climbs have varying amounts of fixed pro, from trad lines with no fixed gear to sport climbs protected entirely by bolts. On some traditional routes, you'll clip the occasional bolt, piton, or stuck piece for protection. A mixed route may have several bolts, with some sections requiring nuts or cams for protection.

Fixed anchors can be totally solid, completely sketchy, or anywhere in between. It's up to you to understand the various types of fixed gear, especially what's bomber and what's not. This knowledge will help you inspect fixed gear to judge how solid it is.

PITONS

On July 4, 1893, William Rogers pounded wooden wedges up the basalt cracks of Devils Tower in Wyoming to build a ladder to the summit. These are still in place, but you wouldn't want to climb on them anymore. Soon thereafter, climbers started using soft steel pitons. They were stronger than the wooden wedges, but they deformed with use and quickly became trashed. In the 1960s, Yvon Chouinard developed hard steel pitons that could be driven and removed repeatedly. These were used to pioneer scores of early free and aid routes. You still find old fixed pitons scattered around in many traditional climbing areas.

One of the keys to a solid piton placement is having a good fit, so pitons come in many sizes. Knifeblades can be bomber or sketchy. The problem is, when they're fixed, you can't tell how long they are or how corroded. Knifeblades range from 1.3 millimeters (0.05 inch) to 3.2 millimeters (0.13 inch) thick. Angle pitons are bent midway along their long axis so they fit wider cracks. They come in several sizes to fit cracks 1.3–4 centimeters (0.5–1.5 inches). Big cams have made bongs nearly obsolete, but you still find a few out on the cliffs. If the clipping eye is damaged, you can sling the bong like a chockstone.

Pitons are tough to evaluate. This piton in a vertical crack may be long or short, new or corroded; you can't tell.

A piton set in a horizontal crack is usually better than one in a vertical crack because it will tend to cam inside the crack rather than rotate out.

Fixed pitons can be helpful, especially in sections where the route has no cracks big enough to accept chocks or cams. The problem is that it can be difficult to judge how solid a fixed piton is: it might be totally bomber or pitifully weak.

Before trusting a fixed piton, visually inspect the rock, the placement, and the piton's condition to learn as much as you can. Tap the piton with a carabiner if you want to learn more: a hollow thud means it's not well set, while a high-pitched ring means it's sitting tight. Inspect the piton for rust or other signs of corrosion, cracks, and structural damage; but remember, the worst corrosion is often inside the crack, where it's impossible to see. If you're uncertain, back up the pin with a good cam or nut if possible.

Sometimes fixed pitons are superfluous, set in cracks that easily accept chocks or cams. In these situations, it's often better to set your own protection or to clip the piton as well as your own gear. Occasionally you can use a fixed piton to help prevent a nut from being wriggled free by the climbing rope.

Setting a Piton

Most climbers today will never need to set a piton. However, for difficult aid climbing or establishing new routes, piton skills can still be important. To set a piton, find a horizontal crack or a placement where the crack narrows above and below. Choose a piton that will slide easily into the crack for about two-thirds of the piton length, then pound it with a hammer until it stops

You can increase the strength of some pitons by tying them off to reduce leverage.

A. Make a coil in the webbing.

B. Push the webbing through itself to make a slipknot.

C. Place the slipknot over the head of the piton, slide it flush against the wall, and cinch it tight.

A fixed piton can be rigged to oppose a nut and help hold it in place.

A. If the two pieces are close together, tie their carabiners into the same clove hitch.

B. If the pieces are farther apart, tie them together with two separate clove hitches. You can also tension the piton and nut against one another by opposing them as shown in chapter 1. (Note: This will increase the force on the nut, due to the pulley effect.)

63

moving deeper with each hammer blow. Overdriving a piton can make the placement weaker by damaging the rock around it. If the piton will become fixed protection, try to find an ideal placement where you can drive it home until the eye just protrudes from the rock; if your partner will remove it, set the piton just enough for your needs in order to minimize rock damage. Listen to the piton as you drive it. A ringing ping that increases in pitch as you hammer means the piton is finding a solid home. A dull thud means the rock around the piton is rotten or hollow.

BOLTS

John Otto pounded steel rods into drilled holes to make his 1911 ascent of Independence Monument in Colorado National Monument. This gargantuan pioneering effort was among the first that involved drilling holes and setting bolts for anchoring on a rock face. Now bolts have proliferated at climbing areas around the world.

Bolts can be a touchy subject. To some climbers, a line of bolts is an enticing vertical path; to others, bolts are an eyesore, an example of poor climbing style, or even an environmental travesty. When bolted sport climbs first arrived on the American climbing scene in the 1980s, the ensuing bolt wars divided the climbing community. Bolts were placed, chopped, replaced, and re-chopped, and friends became enemies. The real loser was the rock, which is still scarred in some areas. Fortunately, most climbers have moved past bolting

controversies, though areas of contention still exist.

Types of Bolts

Most bolts used for climbing in North America are mechanical bolts originally designed by the construction industry for fastening structures to concrete and stone. The bolts are coupled with a hanger so that climbers can clip carabiners to the anchor. Two styles of expansion bolts are prevalent: the five-piece bolt and the wedge bolt. Both styles are available in carbon steel, or, for

The proliferation of bolts over the last thirty years has allowed many climbing areas and routes to be created that would otherwise be too dangerous or unpleasant to climb.

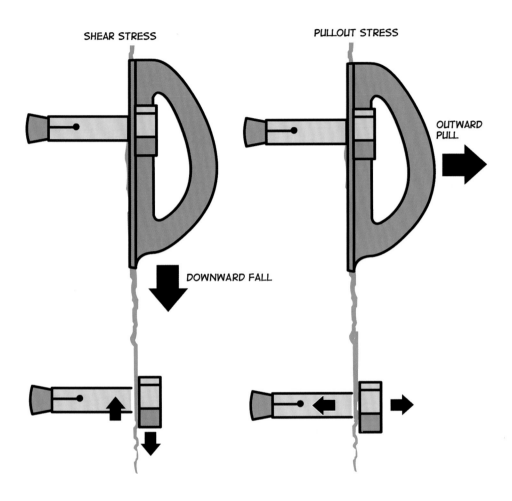

SHEAR STRESS

PULLOUT STRESS

OUTWARD
PULL

DOWNWARD FALL

Bolt stress. A bolt needs high shear strength to resist pulls perpendicular to its axis and good pullout strength to resist forces along its axis. A fall on a vertical wall or slab creates mostly shear stress on a bolt, though a climber who pitches outward in a fall will also create some pullout force. A team hanging at an anchor station and leaning out creates both shear- and pullout stress on the anchors. A bolt set in a horizontal roof will receive mostly pullout stress if the climber falls or hangs on the bolt.

GOOD BOLTS

13-mm (½-inch) diameter 5-piece bolt

10-mm (⅜-inch) diameter wedge bolts

The 13-millimeter (½-inch) five-piece bolts and the 10-millimeter (⅜-inch) wedge bolts make great climbing anchors, provided they are properly placed in solid rock and are not rusted or corroded.

triple the price, stainless steel. Stainless is the better choice in all but the driest climates. To set a mechanical bolt, you drill a hole into the rock, blow out the rock dust, fix the bolt with a hanger, and then pound it into the drilled hole. Tightening the bolt expands it inside the hole to provide good shear- and pullout strength.

Five-piece bolt. Some of the most bomber bolts you'll find are often called five-piece bolts. The actual bolt screws through a metal sleeve into a cone-shaped expander. To set a five-piece bolt, pound the bolt assembly into the drilled hole. Tightening the bolt pulls the expander cone into the metal sleeve, which expands the sleeve. Further tightening pushes the end of the bolt through the expander cone, which expands its four sections to undercut the rock near the base of the hole. This gives the bolt tremendous pullout strength. The bolt itself can actually be unscrewed and removed, while the sleeve and expander remain fixed in the hole.

Wedge bolt. Wedge bolts are somewhat easier to place than five-piece bolts, especially when set on lead. Tightening a wedge bolt pulls the wedge cone into the expansion cylinder, which expands to lock the bolt in the hole.

Glue-in bolt. Glue-in bolts are abundant in some areas and rare in others. They are the best choice for sea cliffs and corrosive rock (some limestone contains elements that rapidly corrode bolts). The one-piece bolt-and-hanger design prohibits the galvanic corrosion that occurs between dissimilar metals (as in a standard bolt with a separate hanger), plus the glue can provide a barrier between the rock and the bolt. The epoxy that glues the bolt into the hole gives it great pullout strength—provided the epoxy is applied correctly. Most glue-in bolts are stainless steel. The most corrosion-resistant of all bolts is a glue-in bolt made from titanium that was designed specifically for use on sea cliffs.

BAD BOLTS

The bolts shown here were commonly used from the 1950s through the 1980s to protect climbs. Several groups have launched noble efforts to replace these dangerous bolts with modern ones, but plenty of old bolts can still be found in some climbing areas. They are not trustworthy: they're too thin, too short, and most have been sitting in the rock for two to five decades.

Bolts in marine climates are especially susceptible to corrosion, as are bolts in wet limestone. In some cases, bolts in place less than three years failed under mere body weight. The culprit seems to be the salty air and sea spray, combined with corrosive minerals from the rock (some limestone seems to be particularly bad). The process is accelerated in sunny areas with high temperatures. Unfortunately, the corrosion may not be visually obvious.

Don't trust bolts that are

- smaller than 10 millimeters (3/8 inch) in diameter,
- rusty or corroded (some forms of corrosion are invisible),
- loose,
- set in bad rock, or
- equipped with a funky homemade hanger.

DANGER

¼-inch wedge bolt

¼-inch button-head

⅜-inch Star Dryvin

DANGER

DANGER

The 6.5-millimeter (¼-inch) wedge bolt, 6.5-millimeter (¼-inch) buttonhead, and 10-millimeter (3/8-inch) Star Dryvin bolts are outdated and unreliable.

This sea-cliff bolt is totally rusted and untrustworthy. Some corrosion is invisible and impossible to detect.

This bolt shows only the slightest tinge of rust on the outside, however, the part of the bolt inside the rock is not visible and could be badly corroded. Avoid trusting your life to a single bolt.

HANGERS

The basic bolt hanger is a stamped piece of stainless steel with a 90-degree bend. One side of the bend has a hole for the bolt, and the other is cut out for clipping. A good hanger has the edges of the cutout rounded so they don't gouge carabiners.

A modern bolt with a standard bolt hanger camouflaged to reduce visual impact—keep your eyes sharp.

Welded cold shuts were popular at one time because you can clip them like any bolt hanger or run your rope through the hanger for rappelling if necessary. They have fallen out of favor due to inconsistent welds and the simplicity and reliability of the standard hanger design.

Glue-ins are considered the strongest bolts, and on sea cliffs, titanium glue-in bolts are best because the glue provides a barrier between the stone and the metal and titanium resists corrosion best, but even these don't last forever. The glue must be mixed correctly, and even with glue-in bolts, it is best to avoid trusting a single one with your life.

EXERCISE—NATURAL ANCHORS

On your next few climbs, seek out natural anchors, whether you're leading or setting top-rope or belay anchors. Find the natural protection that makes sense and incorporate it into your protection system. Some climbing areas offer more natural protection opportunities than others.

Opposite: *Silvia Luebben in the moment on* Max Factor *(5.11c), Vedauwoo, Wyoming*

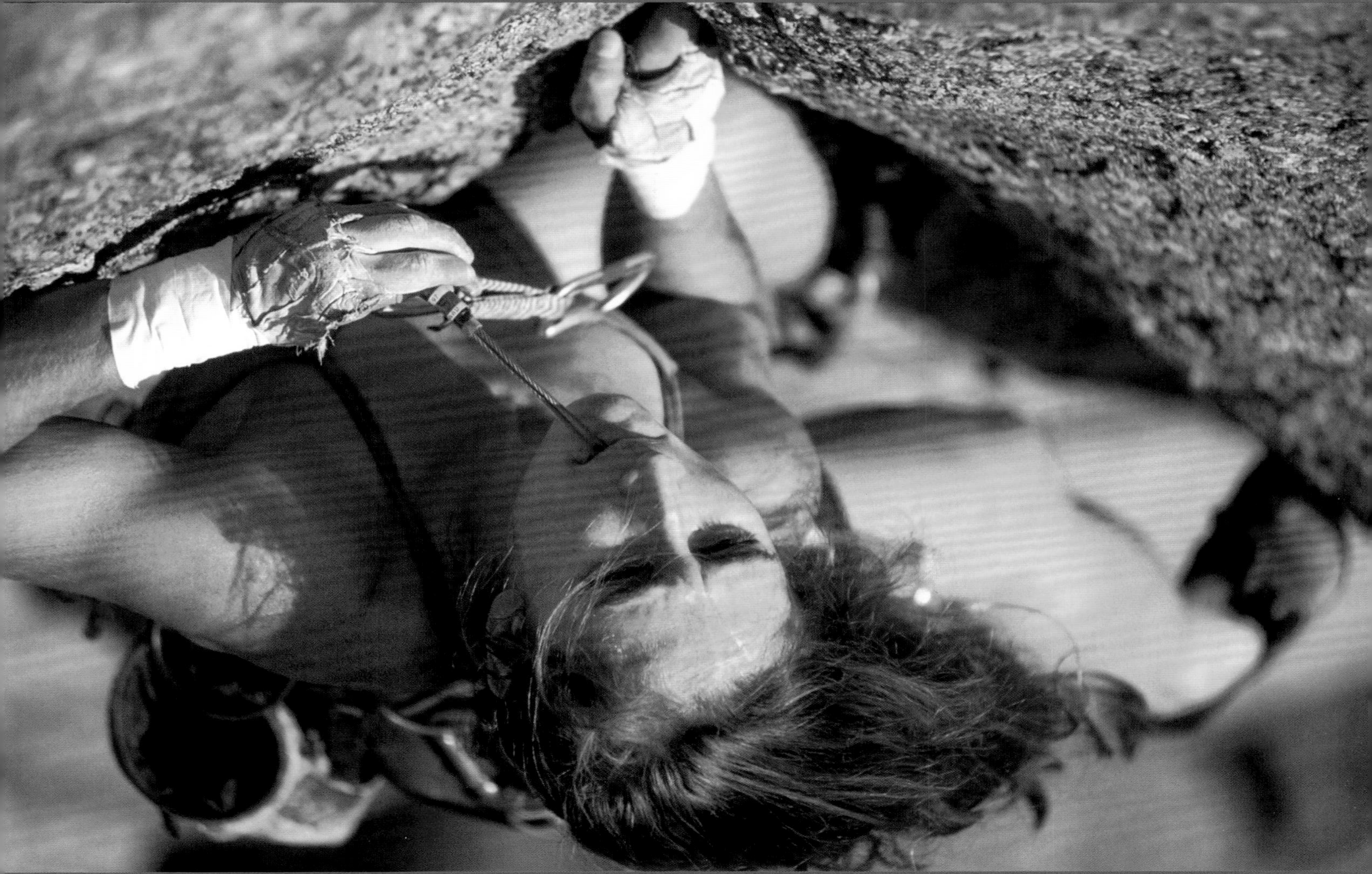

CHAPTER 3

Chocks

One of the bastions of traditional climbing, the Shawangunks in New York, was discovered for rock climbing by Fritz Wiessner in the 1930s. He soon opened a number of routes up to 5.7, a respectable difficulty given the era and the primitive gear. *Modern Times* is one of the classics, opened in the 1960s. It follows the typical horizontally banded quartz conglomerate, busting through big roofs on big holds.

A well-used set of chocks always has some stories to tell.

You definitely want a good selection of cams on *Modern Times*; they work best when the horizontal cracks are parallel and when you need to set the gear quickly. But you'll also carry wired nuts and possibly some Tricams or hexes. These provide bomber placements in spots where the cracks waver, where the horizontal cracks are lipped, and where regular cams don't fit well or at all. They also work at the belay, so you can save the precious cams for the lead.

This chapter covers all the types of protection other than cams, including

- wired nuts,
- micronuts,
- hexes,
- Tricams,
- slider nuts,
- Big Bros.

For each type of anchor, we'll discuss

- pros and cons,
- how to set and remove the anchor,
- how to evaluate the placement.

Technically, Tricams, slider nuts, and Big Bros are cams because of the way they transfer a downward pulling force into a horizontal force against the crack walls, but they are included here so that spring-loaded camming units can have their own chapter. Most of the chocks might also be considered *passive protection*, because they have no moving parts. Cams and slider nuts fall into the *active protection* category because the spring actively holds the protection in place. Big Bros have moving parts and a spring, and they are held in the crack by pressure from the locking collar, so they are also active protection.

EVOLUTION OF CLIMBING CHOCKS

Pitons were the predominant climbing anchors for many years. Each piton placement chipped some rock away, though, and in time, the popular routes became pitifully scarred. Years later, you can still find these piton scars on the old classic routes. In fact, the scars create the finger jams and pockets on many modern free climbs.

British climbers began the movement toward "clean climbing" that required no hammer and did not scar the rock. They started by tying slings around chockstones for protection. As early as 1926, some clever Brits stuffed their pockets with stones to jam in the cracks and tie off for protection. Eventually, they scavenged machine nuts along the railroad tracks, filed out the threads, and slung the holes with cord. Soon enough, they were drilling holes in the larger nuts to save weight. Armed with racks of machine nuts, they

A selection of early chocks

tackled increasingly difficult climbs. In the early 1960s, they began making nuts specifically for climbing. They experimented with many exotic shapes: truncated cones, pyramids, knurled cylinders, and T- and H-shaped bars. Ultimately, the wedge and hexagonal shapes emerged as the most practical due to their good stability and high strength-to-weight ratio.

Most climbers resisted clean climbing—at first. They trusted their pitons, and they weren't going to trust a chunk of metal slotted in a crack. Pitons probably would have held their ground, except that slotting nuts is much easier than banging pitons. Once climbers realized this, they dumped their heavy hammers and iron for light nuts and hex-shaped chocks made of aircraft aluminum.

The most versatile nut, the Tricam, was invented by Greg Lowe in 1973 and came to market in 1981. Tricams are unique because they can jam in a constriction like a wedge or cam in a parallel crack. Tricams have a cult of followers who always carry a few small Tricams. They swear by Tricams, while others swear at them. Tricams work great in many situations, but the larger sizes never caught on because they lack the stability of spring-loaded cams. There's nothing worse than having your protection fall out well below your feet.

The first commercially successful cams, called Friends, appeared in 1978. As cams took over, larger chocks (bigger than finger-size) took the back seat. A climber might carry large chocks, but only to supplement a set or two of cams. Wired nuts have held their ground, though. They remain the warhorse for protecting thin cracks.

Climbers experimented with sliding nuts, double wedges sliding against one another to lock in a crack (similar to the way a doorstop works) as early as 1946. Finally, in 1983 they became available when Doug Phillips introduced Sliders. The design was improved when Steve Byrne invented ball nuts, which have a ball that rotates in a groove to accommodate mildly flaring cracks.

Craig Luebben designed Big Bro expandable tube chocks, with help from Chuck Grossman and mechanical engineering professor Jaime Cardenas-Garcia, in 1984. The name comes from George Orwell's book *1984* and the line "Big Brother is watching you." Big Bros came to market in 1987, extending protection into the realm of off-widths and squeeze chimneys—anything from 8 to 30.5 centimeters (3.2 to 12 inches).

WIRED NUTS

Wired nuts are indispensable on many traditional climbs. They work wonders jamming in the constrictions of small, irregular cracks. Because they are small and light, you can carry a bunch of them. They're cheap, too, at least compared to cams. Losing some wired nuts to bail off a route won't leave you crying.

Wired nuts come in many sizes, ranging from 3.8 to 50 millimeters (0.15 to 2 inches). They work great in the small to medium sizes, but hexagonal chocks or Tricams may be a better choice for passive protection for cracks wider than 25 millimeters (1 inch).

SETTING NUTS

When seeking a spot in the crack to set a nut, look for the following:

- **Solid rock surrounding the nut.** Fractured, rotten, friable, or soft rock may shatter under load.
- **Constrictions** that jam the nut against a downward pull and ideally against an outward tug too.
- **A good fit.** Choose the right size of nut to best fit the crack. If the nut doesn't fit

GOOD

A bomber nut placement resists an outward pull, has good surface contact with the rock on both sides, and would require significant rock or metal deformation to move under a downward pull.

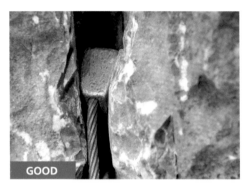

GOOD

In softer rock, try to place nuts with more rock between the nut and potential failure. Here, in limestone, the nut is placed deeper in the crack than might be necessary in granite.

DANGER

This nut would be stronger with more surface contact.

DANGER

This nut has poor contact on the left side. If just a little rock breaks, it's outta there!

DANGER

This endwise nut is strong in a downward pull but could be easily knocked loose or fall out. If this is the best you can find, clip it with a long sling to minimize the rope action from knocking it out and climb past carefully without pulling outward on it.

well, try the next size. If you're setting a curved nut, orient the concave face to the right or left so it best fits the crack, striving for maximum surface contact between the nut and the rock.

Think **R**ock **DOG**:

- The **R**ock must be solid.
- The crack should have constrictions to oppose a **D**ownward pull and ideally an **O**utward pull.
- The nut should have a **G**ood fit in the crack.

If the nut fits well, you can usually just place it gently in the crack. Your partners will appreciate it. Sometimes a light tug helps set the nut. The amount of force you can exert by tugging will not even come close to the force of a fall, so don't consider pulling on a nut to be a test. Occasionally, it's wise to set the nut with a sharp tug (or a few) to keep it from lifting out due to climber movement. If the placement can be easily lifted out by an outward pull and you can't find a better spot, or if it's the last good piece for a while and you absolutely need

Cleaning chocks:
You can push, prod, poke, or pull with a nut tool to liberate stubborn nuts. Some climbers rig the nut tool with a keeper cord to prevent dropping it, but others find the cord easily tangles with other gear and the benefit of the cord isn't worth the hassle.

When the nut has a hole in the side, try inserting the nut tool in the hole and lever the nut to loosen it.

If the nut refuses to budge, hold the working end of the nut tool against the stuck nut and smack the other end with a large chock, rock, or carabiner, but be careful not to drop anything on climbers below.

SIDE VIEW   TOP VIEW

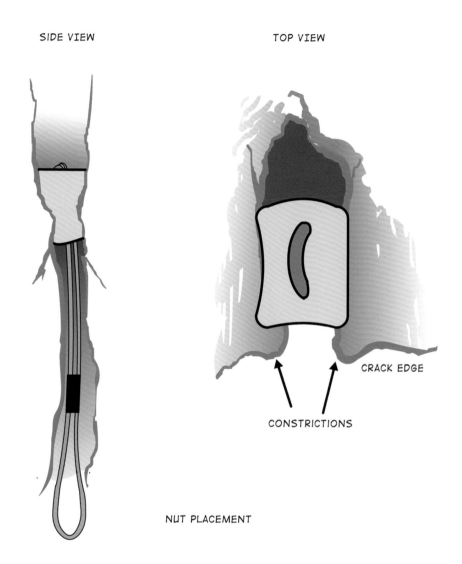

CRACK EDGE

CONSTRICTIONS

NUT PLACEMENT

If you can find downward and outward constrictions and fit them with the right size nut, you'll have a secure placement.

the nut to stay in place, then go ahead and yank it. Save this bullying technique for crucial times, though; your partners will hate cleaning a pitch full of yanked, stuck nuts.

CLEANING NUTS

To remove a nut, imagine the path it took going into the crack. Usually it's obvious, but sometimes the nut was wriggled

Most climbers prefer the nuts they practice with the most. Tapered nuts fit better in flares, where parallel-sided nuts will often be insecure. Experienced climbers use both. Brass nuts tend to bite the rock better, but steel nuts are more durable and less prone to deformation under extreme loads.

through some intricate maze that must be retraced to free the piece. Hold the cables and try to wriggle the nut loose, then work it out through the opening. If it won't budge, you might try whipping the cable upward with the carabiner to loosen it; overusing this practice, though, will bend and eventually fray a nut's cables, and it also might get the nut more stuck.

Sometimes a nut gets really stuck, especially if the leader fell or hung or set it with a yank. If the nut won't budge, break out the nut tool.

SHAPE AND FIT

A good fit maximizes the surface-contact area between the nut and the rock, decreasing the pressure on the rock and adding strength and stability to the placement. Nuts are available in different shapes to help you find the best fit for a given crack. Curved nuts have a concave face on one side and a convex face on the other; they fit securely in many tapering placements and are the favorites of many climbers. Straight-sided nuts have no curve, but they fit many cracks well, and they get stuck less than curved nuts. Offset nuts fit flared cracks and piton scars, making them especially useful for aid climbing and for protection in areas with flaring cracks and piton scars.

Climbers often place mediocre protection that could be much better with just a minor adjustment—sometimes moving the piece only a few millimeters vastly improves the placement. Use special care to find the best fit.

OKAY

In a pinch, you can set a nut endwise to fit a bigger crack, but it's weaker. In solid rock, sideways placements are often bomber because the wide surfaces against the rock result in more surface contact.

OKAY

In a horizontal crack, try to find an opening in the back of the crack that allows you to slide the nut toward a constriction on the edge of the crack. Such a placement can be bomber. The piece shown is good, provided it does not get pulled to the left.

DANGER

The crack has no constriction to resist an outward pull, so the rope may wriggle the nut out, or the nut might pop out in a fall. Even worse, it has very poor surface contact with the rock. If the rock breaks a little, the nut will fail.

DANGER

This nut could pull the fractured block on the left side loose. Be careful what you set your anchors behind. The nut also relies on a thin, fractured layer on the right side.

MICRONUTS

Micronuts fit the tiniest cracks, but they have limited strength—the nuts, wires, and contact area with the rock are small. The smallest micronuts are intended for aid placements only, or perhaps to oppose a larger nut and hold it in place. In a good placement in solid rock, larger micronuts can be strong enough to catch *most* falls.

Traditional micronuts are made of brass, with a stainless-steel cable silver-soldered to the nut. The soldering avoids a sharp bend in the cable and fills the holes drilled for inserting the cable, which maximizes the strength of the small nut. Some micronuts are made of copper-infused steel, which provides strength and grip with the rock surface.

Micronuts are used for tiny cracks. Pay attention to the kN ratings on micronuts—the middle and larger sizes are surprisingly strong, while the smaller ones can break in a short fall.

This micronut is too close to the edge of the crack, and it's barely touching on the left side.

This micronut has poor surface contact on the right side. A slight outward tug in a fall or a little rope wriggle will free it from the crack.

GOOD

Here, a nest of two micronuts was placed to maximize the strength and compensate for potential uncertainty due to not being able to see into the small crack to determine the details of the placement. When in doubt, more micronuts are usually better.

GOOD

This micronut is one of the larger sizes, so the tested strength is plenty to hold a fall; it has good surface contact on both sides, and the brass material will help prevent it from dislodging due to rope drag or climber movement. In thin, shallow cracks, consider micronuts with sideways orientations.

EQUALIZING THE LOAD

When setting micronuts, small wired nuts, or any placements of dubious strength, consider setting two and equalizing them so that they share the load to make a stronger anchor.

To get more strength from micronuts or small wired nuts (or other sketchy gear), consider equalizing them with a shoulder-length sling. Don't forget the 180-degree twist in the sling!

In a rare circumstance, you can self-equalize three anchors with a sling. Clip the sling into each of the nuts, pull down a loop of sling between each of the three nuts, and put 180-degree twists in two of the loops. Clip all three loops. Though it's time- and gear-consuming, equalizing small or weak protection increases the chances that it will hold.

HEXAGONAL CHOCKS

Chocks based on a modified hexagonal shape work like normal nuts, only they're designed to fit bigger cracks. The four or five sizes ranging from 2.5 to 6.5 centimeters (1 to 2.5 inches) seem the most practical, though you can buy smaller and larger models. Hexagonal chocks come slung with webbing or cable. The webbing is lighter and stronger, while the cable-slung hexes allow you to reach high placements and are less prone to tangling on the rack.

When placing a hex-shaped chock, find a downward constriction to jam the chock and an outward constriction to hold it in place. Strive for maximum surface contact between the rock and the chock. Hexagonal chocks can cam somewhat in a crack, due to the sling (or cable) position causing a

DANGER

This hex placement looks good at first glance because the crack is tapered nicely; but upon closer inspection, it is not stable because it's set too close to the crack edge, is not rotated to get a snug fit on the planar sides of the piece, and will fall out of the crack with even the slightest outward pull.

GOOD

A bomber hex placement. Hexes are significantly lighter than camming units of the same size.

GOOD

A hex set endwise fits a wider crack.

GOOD

This hex was slipped through an opening into a constriction at the lip of this horizontal crack and not only wedges but also cams to hold it in position. It will hold multidirectional pulls.

rotation of the chock, but no spring exists to hold the chock in place, so they work best when jammed in a constriction. Because of the asymmetric shape, you can fit two crack sizes with a sideways placement, and a third size with an endwise placement.

TRICAMS

Climbers love or hate Tricams, often based on where they climb. Tricams are extremely versatile, with two placement modes: you can wedge a Tricam in a tapering crack just like a nut, or cam it in a parallel crack. Their compact shape allows them to fit in pockets or pods where nothing else can.

Tricams used to be made in eleven sizes, but due to climbers preferring the smaller ones, modern Tricams are made only in the smaller sizes.

A. When camming a Tricam, lay the sling inside the rails. New Tricams have stiffer webbing to facilitate ease of placement and removal.

B. Set the fulcrum (or point) in a divot, microcrack, or small edge inside the crack or pocket for stability. Tug the Tricam to set it and be careful not to wriggle it loose with the rope.

REPLACING WEBBING

Most chocks and camming units come with a sewn webbing sling or swaged cable loop for clipping. Some commercial outfits replace worn slings, or you can tie on your own when the sling gets worn. Use climbing webbing or cord with a strength rating of at least 16 kN (3,600 pounds) for reslinging the gear. Tie the cord into a loop with a double fisherman's, unless the cord manufacturer recommends a triple fisherman's, and tie the webbing with a water knot. Check your water knots each time you use them, as they tend to untie with repeated loading.

When wedging a Tricam in its more passive orientation, find a fit that gives solid surface contact between the Tricam and the rock with a good constriction to hold the Tricam in place.

The new Tricams are also tapered in their sideways orientations, adding versatility to what was already arguably the most versatile protection.

Tricams work very well in pockets, where cams or nuts do not.

This Tricam is unstable because the fulcrum has no rock feature to hold it in place and the crack flares downward.

SLIDING NUTS

Sliding nuts fit parallel cracks from 3 to 16 millimeters (0.12 to 0.63 inch). The semispherical "ball" wedges against the "ramp" like a door on a doorstop. This creates a large outward force that generates friction to oppose a pull. The ball can rotate to adjust for a small amount of flare in the crack. A small camming unit is usually easier to assess than a sliding nut, but the sliding nut will fit smaller cracks.

Right: *Sliding nuts, also called ball nuts, work in tiny parallel cracks where no other protection will work. Like all cams, these are most secure when there is a passive element holding them in the crack, such as a slight constriction, edge, or bump just under the placement.*

To set a ball nut, retract the trigger and insert the piece in a crack, just above a minor constriction if possible. Release the trigger so that the ball jams against the ramp. It should be 50 percent or less expanded and have good surface contact with the rock. Tug the ball nut to test it and set it.

GOOD

This placement looks reasonably good. The piece was extended with a quickdraw (not shown) so the rope wouldn't wriggle the ball nut free.

If you set a ball nut in a less than perfect placement, consider setting two and equalizing them.

EXPANDABLE TUBES

Big Bro expandable tubes cover cracks from 7 to 47 centimeters (2.75 to 18.5 inches). A Big Bro is much lighter and more compact than a giant cam and more stable when set in a good placement. You can't slide the Big Bro up the crack like a cam, though. A giant cam is easier to set than a Big Bro and works better in flared cracks.

Four sizes of Big Bro expandable tubes protect parallel cracks, from fist cracks to small chimneys. Big Bros are lighter and more compact than giant camming units but harder to place.

Big Bros provide anchors in cracks bigger than the largest cam as demonstrated by Big Bro inventor Craig Luebben on the Texas Finger Crack (5.11), Escalante Canyon, Colorado.

To place a Big Bro:

A. Find a parallel spot in the crack and push the inner tube (the side with the collar) against the wall.

B. Push the trigger button so that the tube expands to fit the crack. Don't "dry fire" a Big Bro by pushing the button and letting the inner tube slam against the stop or the rock—instead, let the tube expand slowly.

C. With the spring holding the tube in place, spin the locking collar. It helps to make sure the locking collar is loose and not jammed tight before starting a lead so that it is easy to spin during placement.

D. Crank the collar down tight against the outer tube.

E. Tug sharply on the sling to test the stability and lock the tube in place. Retighten the collar.

F. Clip the rope into the sling with a carabiner.

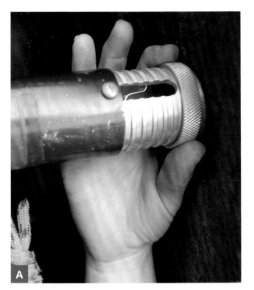

To remove a Big Bro:
A. Spin the collar to the end of the tube.

B. Collapse the unit until the trigger pops up.

Left: If the crack flares, find the most parallel placement possible. Set the cord end so it fully contacts the rock, and let the other side touch in one point, like a Tricam. Use a long sling so the rope doesn't disturb the placement and be careful not to knock it loose as you climb past.

SIZE AND STRENGTH OF CHOCKS

All brands and models of chocks come in a set of complementary sizes, from small to large, and are numbered according to size. This creates a selection for fitting various cracks: if a piece is too small, try the next size up.

It's wise to not trust the tiniest nuts much; even if the nut doesn't break, the rock might. A small nut might slow you down, though, or stop a short fall, especially if you're high up on the pitch so the impact force is low. To increase the odds of nuts holding, consider equalizing two small nuts.

Only nuts thicker than 8–14 millimeters (5/16–½ inch), depending on the brand, rate a full strength of 10 or 12 kN (2,250 to 2,700 pounds), which is sufficient to hold most climbing falls. In these medium and larger sizes, rock quality and placement stability become the important factors for ensuring placement security. One brand of hexagonal chocks rates below full strength in the smallest two sizes (rated 6 kN/1,350 pounds), but most brands rate from 10 to 14 kN (2,250 to 3,150 pounds) throughout the size range.

Sliding nuts are not as strong, ranging from 4.5 to 8 kN (1,000 to 1,800 pounds), depending on the size. Because of their limited strength and fickle nature, use these devices with care. Expandable tubes rate a burly 15 kN (3,375 pounds) across their size range.

EXERCISE—GEAR PLACEMENT

Beginning Trad Climber: Round up an assortment of nuts and chocks, as well as some Tricams, slider nuts, and Big Bros. Find a cliff base with good cracks and no climbers above and set all the different sizes of nuts and chocks. Find placements that lock the pieces in the crack, so they cannot wiggle easily or get pulled out from rope movement. Clip a sling to the pieces and yank on them to test their stability. Pull down and also yank them outward to see if they can handle that direction of pull.

Set a lot of different pieces and try to pick the right size on the first try. Notice how a piece is much more stable with good rock-surface contact, and how a curved nut sometimes fits better if you turn it to face the other way.

Intermediate Trad Climber: This exercise is also a personal challenge. Go to the cliff base with wired nuts and chocks and set some pieces. Before choosing which nut to set in the crack, look at the placement closely and guess which size will fit the best. If you guess on the first try, give yourself one point. Second try, no points; third try or more, negative one. Now set ten pieces. Depending on how intricate the placements are, try to get a score of at least five. If your score is near zero, keep working at it. If you consistently score below zero, you better stick to leading easy routes where you can hang around to fiddle with gear.

Take the same training to your routes. Avoid the tendency to always fire in a cam; instead, keep your mind open to passive protection opportunities. Focus on getting the right size piece on the first try.

Opposite: *Brittany Griffith fires in a cam on* Disco Machine Gun *(5.12), Indian Creek Canyon, Utah.*

CHAPTER 4

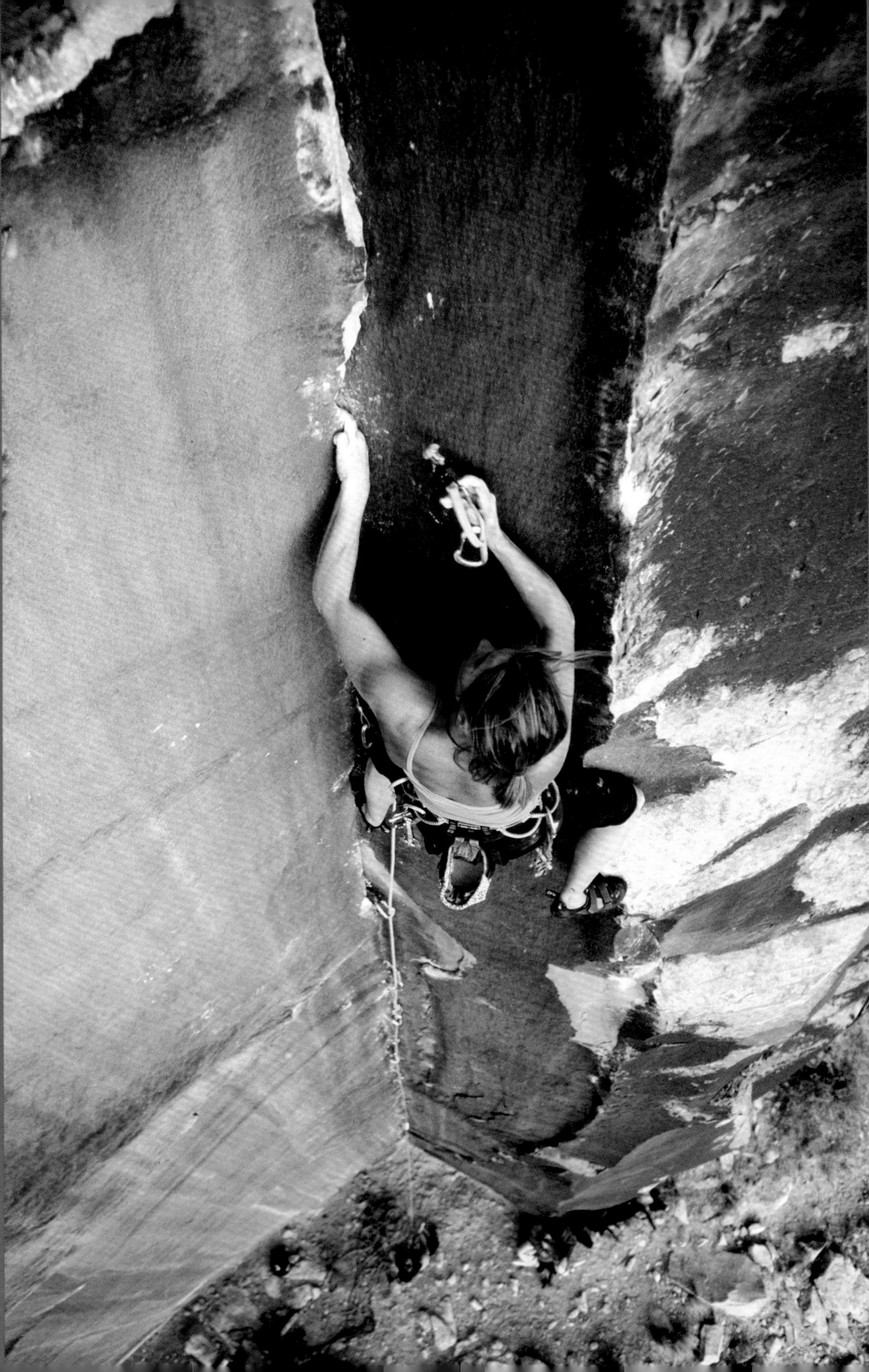

Cams

The ambiance of the desert, combined with the thousands of perfect cracks, makes Indian Creek, Utah, a dream to many climbers. In Indian Creek, the cracks are parallel, and you need cams—a lot of 'em. A single pitch often requires seven or more cams of the same size. This area has single-handedly funded the climbing cam companies.

Leaving the ground, you feel the calm comfort of good jams; you climb high to the first cam, make another good run to the second, then you find a rhythm: jam, jam, jam, jam, set pro, start over.

The first climbers in Indian Creek didn't have any cams. It was the introduction of Friends in 1978 that really set climbers free in Indian Creek and other crack climbing areas. Suddenly, parallel cracks became fast and easy to protect—no more fiddling around with chocks that would just rattle down the crack. Instead, fire the cam in, clip it, and go!

NUTS VERSUS CAMS

The crack often dictates what type of gear to place. Cams work best in parallel cracks, while nuts and hexes work better in convoluted, wavy cracks. Sometimes you have a lot of options for what to set, so you place nuts to save the cams for later.

Wired nuts are light and cheap, so you can carry a bundle of them, and it won't break your budget to leave a few to bail off a route. Nothing goes in fast like a cam, though, a definite plus on hard pitches. A well-set cam also has the ability to swivel and withstand an outward or even upward pull, so cams are good at belays and as the first piece in a pitch. Cams also expand continuously through their expansion range, so they fit any size crack in that range, whereas a nut or hex has only two or three sizes.

This chapter describes

- the evolution of cams for climbing,
- how cams work,
- how to set and remove cams,
- good and bad cam placements,
- tips for freeing stuck cams.

The chapter also discusses key aspects of cam design, including

- cam lobes,
- axles,
- expansion range,
- stem,
- sling,
- color coding.

Cam components of a double-axle cam viewed from above

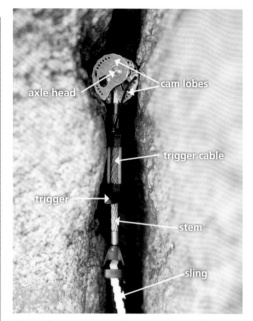

All modern spring-loaded camming devices (SLCDs) have similar components: opposing spring-loaded cam lobes arranged on an axle or axles, with a trigger for retracting the cam lobes when setting or removing the cam. The trigger rides along a flexible stem that also works as a handle for placing the unit. Most cams come with a sewn sling for clipping.

CAM EVOLUTION

The idea of camming first entered the climbing world in 1958, when Swiss guide Adolf Jüsy and engineer Walter Marti introduced jumar rope ascenders for climbing up ropes. Expanding on that idea, Greg Lowe created the Lowe Cam Nuts. They came to market in 1973, making them the first spring-loaded cams designed for anchoring. This design probably influenced Ray Jardine, who developed his Friends in secrecy during the mid-1970s, as he ticked many of Yosemite Valley's first 5.12 routes using his prototypes. He also climbed what was probably the first 5.13 in the world, *The Phoenix*. Friends were introduced to the climbing world in 1978, and they became the first commercially successful camming unit.

When the rigid-stemmed Wild Country Friends came on the market, traditional rock climbing was changed forever. Overnight, parallel cracks that had been a nightmare to climb became easily protectable. Friends were initially available in only three sizes: 1 through 3.

Shortly after Friends became available, other inventors went to work tweaking the design. The cable U-stem pioneered by Steve Byrne and Doug Phillips allowed

The cams that started it all: the original Wild Country Friends. These units are still usable thirty-five years later.

cams to be set in horizontal cracks without risk of breaking the stem, and their TCU (three-cam unit) design enabled camming units to fit into shallow cracks. German climber Stefan Engers introduced the single cable stem with his Jokers in 1985. This flexible stem worked well in many crack configurations, and other companies soon adopted the design.

Dave Waggoner created the internal cam spring design of the Aliens in the mid-1980s. This design provides the strength and security of four cams but allows the cams to fit closer on the axle for placement in shallow cracks. The internal cam spring also sets the cams more directly opposite each other on the axle for improved performance in flared cracks. The same company also created Hybrid Aliens, with two different sizes of cams set on the axle to further accommodate flaring cracks and piton scars.

Inventor Tony Christianson developed the double-axle cam, which was introduced by Chouinard Equipment (later to become Black Diamond) in 1987. The double-axle Camalots offered an increased expansion range, allowing a set of cams to cover a given size range with fewer pieces. This larger expansion range also made it easier to choose the right size of cam for a given placement. In 2006, Black Diamond introduced the C3, a three-cam design for thin cracks. In 2016, Black Diamond's Ultralight Camalots shaved significant weight off the Camalot design by using thinner cams and a stem made of high-strength cord rather than cable. This weight savings comes at the cost of the unit's life span, as the units

CAM PHYSICS

Just how does that camming unit hold a fall? The answer is friction. The precisely calculated curve of the cam face causes the lobes to transform downward force (created by a falling or hanging climber) into an outward force that's twice as great and is directed against the crack walls. By pushing outward so hard, the camming unit creates friction between the cam faces and the crack walls to oppose the downward pull.

Due to the massive potential force on a cam, the rock surrounding the crack needs to be solid—a loose block or flake can easily get pried loose by a loaded camming unit. The rock surface where the cams touch also needs to be solid, not flaky, grainy, gritty, dirty, or lichen-coated. In poor rock, the cams can pulverize the rock grains and pull out.

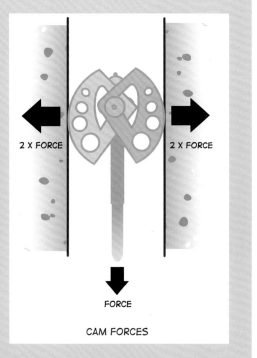

2 X FORCE   2 X FORCE

FORCE

CAM FORCES

Cams can hold even in a slightly flaring crack and sometimes seem to defy physics in how tenacious they can be. Other times a seemingly solid cam will fail under a relatively short fall or even under body weight. The most common culprit for unexpected cam failure is smooth rock. The less grippy the rock is, the less flare angle a cam can endure. In very smooth rock, such as quartzite and metamorphosed sandstone, a cam may not hold even in a parallel crack because there isn't enough friction.

will lose strength at the same rate as any high-strength cord and must be retired as per manufacturer recommendations.

Doug Phillips added the Range Finder system to the Metolius TCUs and Power Cams (from number 2 on up) in the early 2000s. A series of colored dots on the cam lobes helps climbers select the best unit for a given crack size. He also introduced Fat Cams for safer anchoring in soft rock and redesigned the TCUs and Power Cams, as well as the Ultralight Master Cams.

All modern cams are strong and well built, and the designs have been around long enough for any kinks to be worked out. The following photos distinguish between expanded-range cams, soft-rock cams, offset cams, double-axle cams, three cams, and single-axle cams.

Double-axle cams:

DMM Dragon Cam

Black Diamond Camalot Ultralight

Expanded-range cams:

Omega Pacific Link Cam

Metolius Supercam

Single-axle four cams:

 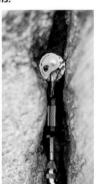  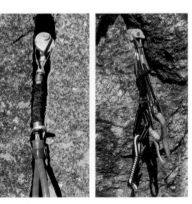

Wild Country Friend

Metolius Ultralight Master Cam

Black Diamond X4

Fixe Alien

Totem Cam

Three cams:

Offset cams:

Soft-rock cams:

| Metolius TCU | Black Diamond C3 | Metolius Offset Master Cam | Fixe Offset Alien | Metolius Fat Cam |

FIXED CHOCKS AND CAMS

Often you'll find stuck nuts and cams, especially on popular classic routes. As long as the sling is not faded and stiff and the piece is not mangled, a fixed piece can be "reasonably" trustworthy—it's up to you to inspect the fixed gear and decide how much to trust it. Clip the cable directly, if possible, to avoid trusting an old sling. A kind leader informs her partner that the gear is fixed if it's not obvious so that the second climber doesn't waste energy and psyche battling to clean a fixed piece.

If you can retrieve a fixed nut or cam, it's your prize to keep. Some climbers have entire racks made of booty. Since you don't know the history, though, it's better not to trust found gear too much. If you decide to climb with the booty, at least inspect the gear closely and replace slings or cords.

SETTING AND REMOVING CAMS

TO SET A CAM

When setting a cam, seek a uniformly parallel spot in the crack, where the crack walls are parallel-sided, not wavering, ridged, bumpy, tapering, or flared downward. You can, and often must, set a camming unit in nonparallel spots, but the best, most predictable placements exist in a parallel or slightly upward-flaring area of the crack.

If you don't have a parallel spot, set the cam above (and below, if possible) a constriction in one of the openings to "trap" the cam and prevent it from walking—such a placement can be very stable. Also avoid placements that rely on a small bump or bulge of rock that could break and cause the cam to pull out or that allow the cam to easily walk.

Cams are stable when they

- open between 10 percent and 50 percent of full expansion,
- open symmetrically, and
- contact solid rock.

TO REMOVE A CAM

Pull the trigger bar to disengage the cams, then remove the piece from the crack. Look

Setting a cam:
A. Find a uniformly parallel spot in the crack where the rock is solid and clean. Choose the right size cam for the crack.
B. Pull the trigger to retract the cam lobes.
C. Insert the unit into the crack, release the trigger so the cams open to fit the crack, and orient the stem to point in the expected loading direction.

at the crack and imagine how the unit went in, then try to work it out through the same path, where the crack is widest. The cam usually comes out easily, but sometimes the leader sets the unit in its tightest configuration, or the cam walks to a tighter position. If the unit feels stuck, pull the trigger harder to fully retract the cam lobes. You may need to slide the cam sideways out of the crack or up or down or wriggle it loose.

If the piece feels stuck, be patient—one hasty move might jam the piece tighter. You may need to hang from the rope or a piece of gear to free both hands for working on the cam. Sometimes, rather than hanging on the rope and blowing your free ascent, you can climb the rest of the pitch free, then lower back down to get the piece.

GOOD

This is a bomber cam placement. The cam lobes are open slightly less than halfway in a section of the crack where the rock tapers slightly below the cam.

When you pull the trigger, try to identify which cam lobe is causing the unit to be stuck (in the worst case, all four cam lobes are jamming). Use your fingers on the cam lobe (or lobes) to help retract them. If the crack is too tight, a nut tool might help retract the individual cam lobes. Keep working the unit (assuming that you have the time to waste on your climb); if the cam lobes can move at all, it's possible to get the cam out. If none of the cam lobes budges, give it up—the piece is fixed.

If you can't reach the trigger bar, take two wired nuts and slide the heads down on the cable (if they are not fixed on the cable). Clip both nuts to a carabiner and use the cable loops to snag each side of the trigger bar (this works better on some models of cams than others). Now pull the carabiner while pushing on the stem or thumb loop to retract the cam lobes.

On many routes, you'll see fixed camming units that someone couldn't remove. These make great booty if you can remove them. Inspect the liberated unit thoroughly before trusting it and always replace the sling.

GOOD AND BAD CAM PLACEMENTS

After you set a cam, check the cam lobes to make sure they all engage the rock so that you have a stable placement. If the placement is not great, retract the trigger and find a more stable spot. Some of the things to look for and to avoid are shown in the pictures on the following pages.

DANGER

Cams placed in flared cracks are unpredictable. This cam may hold a huge fall, or it may fail under body weight, and it's a rare climber who can be sure of the difference. It's better to avoid extremely flaring placements like this one.

DANGER

If you force a camming unit into a tight spot, its cams may jam. When fully compressed, the cams can't get any smaller for removal, so they can become hopelessly stuck in the crack. This cam has two problems: it is almost stuck due to a tight placement, and it is placed on downward-flaring rock which could cause it to fail. A weak cam that is stuck— the worst of both worlds.

DANGER

The crack opens up right below this cam, so if it slips just a little, it's toast.

DANGER

The tie-off high on the stem of this old Friend prevents loading the rigid stem over an edge. Unlike a cable stem, it won't get kinked from repeated loading in horizontal cracks, but these rigid-stem cams are now beyond their recommended life span.

DANGER

This rigid-stemmed cam might break on the rock edge if it takes a hard load. The placement would be better if it were set deeper in the crack to reduce leverage on the stem.

OKAY

A camming unit set in a horizontal crack. A hard fall might kink the cables, but a well-placed unit will still hold the fall. Horizontal placements are somewhat less predictable than vertical ones, however.

thin flake

DANGER

A cam generates twice as much outward force as the downward load it holds, so in a fall it can easily pry off a block or flake or even break the edge of a thin flake like this. The falling rock could injure you, your partner, your rope, or all three.

OKAY

This crack flares quite a bit—the cam may or may not hold. Because the rock has good friction, the placement may be okay, but you wouldn't want this to be the only thing between you and the emergency room.

OKAY

This microcam (size 000) can protect sections of climbing that used to require pitons or were dangerously runout, but because the smallest cams fit cracks that are usually too small to see into, it can be difficult to evaluate the placement.

CAM TESTING

In 1994, Craig Luebben conducted a number of strength tests on cams set in good granite and soft sandstone. These tests were conducted with a slow-pull machine, which is more severe than the fast loading and unloading in a real fall. In most tests, the units failed at loads between 12.5 and 14 kN (2,800 to 3,100 pounds)—plenty strong enough to hold most real-life falls. The strongest cam managed to hold around 19 kN (4,250 pounds) before it exploded through the soft sandstone rock; at this point the axle was severely deformed.

The weakest cam, however, held about 0.5 kN (115 pounds) before it broke a thin sandstone flake. Other cams failed at frighteningly low loads near or below 4 kN (900 pounds) if (a) the cam lobes were open too wide, (b) the piece was set in a flare in soft sandstone, (c) the piece was set near the edge of the crack in soft sandstone, or (d) the piece was set behind a loose block. A smart climber avoids placements like these.

In the soft sandstone, many of the cams punched through the harder surface layer at around 7 kN (1,600 pounds). Once this happened, the cams would continue pulverizing the surface layer and slide out of the crack. When leading on soft sandstone, you're wise to set the cams fairly close together to minimize the length of a fall and the force created and to have ample backup below in case a piece does fail. Belay anchors should also be well equalized. Another way to increase anchor strength in soft sandstone is to use Fat Cams, which have cam lobes that are much thicker than most other units. These spread the load over a wider surface area of rock, which decreases the pressure on the crack walls.

CAM DESIGN

Any cam design is a balancing act: weight against strength, "holding power" against expansion range, durability against cost. To choose the best cams, decide how you will use them and what features are most useful. Don't base your decision solely on dollars; it's better to choose the cams that provide the most security and utility for the lightest weight.

CAM LOBES

Cam lobes are the heart of a cam. The lobes' curvature is designed to create the same cam interception angle (the angle between a line drawn from the axle to where the cam contacts the rock and a line perpendicular to the crack wall—see drawing on next page—throughout a cam's expansion range. A smaller cam angle creates greater outward force on the crack wall, which increases its chances of holding in a flare, slick rock, or other irregular placement. Increasing the cam angle adds expansion range, but if the cam angle is too greedy, the unit won't create enough friction to hold. Most cam companies have settled on a cam angle around 13.75 degrees.

When pull-tested in a lab, cams are generally set in a perfect parallel placement in a testing jig, with the stem aligned exactly along the direction of pull. A force is applied and progressively increased until

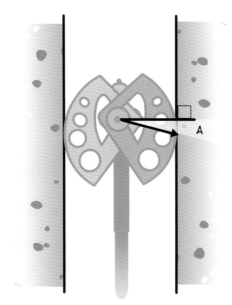

A= CAM INTERCEPTION ANGLE

The curvature of the cam lobes determines their interception angle with the rock.

the unit fails. While the constant force during a pull test can be harsher than the split-second loading of an actual leader fall, in real rock the placements are often not perfect. The crack may be flared, or the stem may not align with the direction of pull, which can create higher stress on the cams. For this reason, some companies overbuild their cams, making them stronger than they need to be for the perfect pull in a testing lab. On the other extreme, cams with large cutouts in the cam lobes may be light, but they may crumple during a bad fall. The UIAA requires only 5 kN (1,125 pounds) in a strength test to certify cams,

which is well below worst-case loading in a leader fall.

Most camming units have four cam lobes, which spread the load over two contact points on each side of the crack. Four cams offer stability in most placements, but if the rope wriggles the piece, the four cams can "walk" inside the crack. When the stem gets rotated up, the outer two cams walk deeper into the crack; when the stem rotates down, the inner two cams walk. If the unit gets rotated back and forth, it can walk progressively deeper into the crack. When this happens, the cams can become so tight that they get stuck, the trigger can bury itself beyond reach, or the cam lobes can open and become unstable. Set a long sling on cams that you suspect might walk to prevent the rope from wriggling them when leading. In a uniformly parallel crack, a small amount of walking potential is usually fine, and unavoidable if the cam is moved at all by rope or the climber as she moves past.

Some companies offer three-cam units (commonly known as TCUs) in the smaller sizes: a single cam on one side of the axle opposes two cams on the other side. With only three cams taking up space on the axle, TCUs can squeeze into shallow cracks. TCUs are also less prone to walking than four-cam models. The middle cam lobe does concentrate the pressure on one side of the crack wall, though, so companies make the middle cam lobe significantly thicker than the two opposing cams to distribute force and partially alleviate this problem.

EXPANSION RANGE

Some of the newest cams offer unprecedented expansion range so that a unit fits in a wider range of crack sizes. Greater expansion makes it easier to choose the right size for the crack; it also improves a cam's performance in flares because the back cams can be closed tight while the front cams are still open pretty wide (like a hybrid cam). The big expansion range allows you to carry fewer cams on some routes, but on a rope-stretching pitch that eats twenty cams, lighter units will give you a fighting chance.

Most companies list a cam's absolute expansion in their promotional literature (cam lobes fully retracted to fully open), which is misleading. Ideally the cam lobes should sit between about 10 percent and 50 percent expanded; in a pinch, you can squeak out a slightly larger placement or squeeze the cam tighter. Set a cam fully retracted, though, and your partner is likely to spend an hour trying to retrieve it—or worse, leave it fixed in the crack. Leave the lobes open too wide, in the cam's larger expansion range, and the cam will be unstable and may walk or pull out in a fall.

Expansion range	
Standard cams	1:1.5
Double-axle cams	1:1.6 to 1:1.7
Supercam	1:1.8
Link cam	1:2.5

This list shows the ratio from cams fully retracted to cams fully open for the various cam designs. The true "safe" expansion ratio is somewhat less than shown because cams should always be placed at less than full expansion.

Some companies mill grooves into the cam lobes' contact surface (where the cam meets the rock). The grooves do not help the actual camming performance, but they can grip small crystals or texture on the rock surface to add stability to the placement. They also may allow a space for tiny broken rock fragments to settle in a hard pull, so the cam lobe can still contact solid rock.

The thickness of the cam lobes' contact faces determine how much pressure they will exert where the cam lobes meet the crack wall. A thicker cam lobe decreases pressure on the rock by spreading the load over more rock surface, reducing the chance of rock failure. A thicker cam lobe also weighs more. Most models of cams have lobes that are about 6-millimeters (¼-inch) thick.

Early models of cams had cam lobes that could invert in a hard pull if the cams were open too wide—both cams would flop over the axle like a blown-out umbrella. Most modern cams have some sort of stop that prevents the cams from inverting, which creates a little more security when the cam is set at its absolute widest range or when placed chock-style in a constriction. Some cam stops also add thickness to the cams when they're near full retraction, so you get more surface contact with the rock in the cam's smaller size range.

AXLES

Most camming units have cam lobes mounted on a single axle, but the double-axle design increases expansion range, and now several companies have double-axle models.

STEM

Virtually all cams made today have flexible stems that bend to reduce leverage when loaded in a horizontal placement. A single cable stem will also bend in a vertical placement if the stem is not aligned with the direction of pull. A single stem can slightly reduce a cam's tendency to walk because the stem's flexibility absorbs wriggle from the rope. Adding a longer sling to the placement, however, works better.

Some models of cams have a U-stem, which bends well when the cam is placed in a horizontal orientation but is not as flexible in a vertical alignment. U-stem units can be more prone to walking when set in a vertical crack but can realign as a fall's force comes onto the cam. The U-stem also protects the trigger cables from wear and kinking, provides rigidity when you're stretching for a faraway placement, and furnishes a high clip-in point for aid climbing.

The U-stem also allows the cam lobes to sit closer on the axle, enabling them to fit narrow placements. In bigger sizes, though, close cam lobes are less stable; most climbers find the U-stem most beneficial in the smaller sizes.

Rigid-stemmed Friends are no longer made, but due to their durability, there are still a lot in use. This design tends to be more durable than cams with flexible stems (because the flexible stem also allows the small trigger wires to move more and eventually break), and they load more predictably, but they should not be set with the stem protruding over the edge of a horizontal or diagonal crack.

Some lightweight designs are now using Spectra/Dyneema as an integral part of the stem design. While this offers reduced weight, the loss of strength over time will be steeper than a unit with a cable stem. Older units with Spectra/Dyneema stems should be thrown away and not "saved for Indian Creek, where I place my cams close together anyway" like so many climbers do with older metal-stemmed cams. A metal-stemmed cam will lose strength at a much slower rate and even after twenty years (long past its recommended life span) will retain much of its original tested strength, provided the sling is replaced regularly. Most manufacturers recommend cams be retired after ten years.

TRIGGER BAR AND THUMB CATCH

Climbing already exacts enough of a toll on our fingers—we don't need our cams adding to the misery. Fortunately, most cams have a fairly ergonomic and digit-friendly trigger design. A stem loop surrounding the thumb catch decreases the chance that you'll drop the cam (especially when wearing gloves for alpine climbing) and allows a place for short-clipping when you're aid climbing. Textured grips make it easier to hang on to a unit when you're pumped or when the air oozes with humidity. Try triggering each size of a model of cams before buying to make sure the trigger system fits your hand—some designs are not great for climbers with small hands.

SLING

Some companies use strong, durable, and highly cut-resistant Spectra/Dyneema.

The extra strength afforded by this high-tech material allows for a lighter, thinner sling to be used but at an additional expense over nylon. Nylon slings are more susceptible to snagging and wear but less costly.

OFFSET CAMS

A couple of companies offer camming units with two different sizes of cams mounted on the axle. You can set the smaller cam lobes deep in the crack while the larger cam lobes sit on the outside for a good fit in a flared crack. These are somewhat specialized, but they work great in flared cracks and piton scars and are especially useful for aid climbing.

Some cams, like the double-axle Dragon Cam, come with an extendable sling that can be clipped shorter or longer to help with rope-drag management.

In a perfect world, climbing companies would standardize the color-coding system so that you could easily identify a cam's size no matter what brand you use, but unfortunately most companies have decided to use their own color scheme.

With practice, you'll learn the color-coding system and eventually relate a certain color to the type of jam you get in the crack. With even more experience, you'll be able to simply look at the crack and pick the right size cam.

Many climbers get so accustomed to their brand and color of cams that they have trouble adjusting to a different brand. To develop confidence beyond the brand, try climbing on other people's gear when possible, and look at the cam lobes themselves to identify the size rather than only the color of the sling.

GIANT CAMS

Giant camming units protect off-width cracks. They're heavy and cumbersome, but you can slide them up a nasty gash to maintain overhead protection as you lead, and they work well in mildly flared wide cracks. Sling the unit with a quickdraw or long sling when leading above the cam, because a giant cam easily walks and tips into a sketchy position if the rope wriggles it. You'll want to carry these unwieldy things only when you know you'll need them.

Big cams can become unstable and flop over, especially when set in their larger size range or when set at the lip of a roof, like this cam on Lucille (5.12), Vedauwoo, Wyoming.

DANGER

Andy Johnson pushing his big cam up Big Pink *(5.11), Vedauwoo, Wyoming*

EXERCISE—CAM SCHOOL

Beginning Trad Climber: Round up all the cams you can, at least a full set, and head to a cliff that has cracks at the base (and no climbers above). Practice placing the different sizes of cams and, if possible, get a guide or experienced climber to check your placements. Yank the sling downward and pull it up to see if the cam rotates to hold the new pull. Practice setting many cams; look closely at the crack width and try to correctly choose which size cam to set on the first try.

Intermediate Trad Climber: Take a bunch of cams to the cliff base and set ten of them as fast as you can. You get one point if you pick the right size on the first try, no points for the second try, and minus one for three or more tries. A score above five means that you have a decent eye for setting cams, but you can still get better. A score near zero means keep practicing.

Advanced Trad Climber: Next time you're looking up a pitch where the crack is largely visible from the ground, take a couple of minutes on the ground and attempt to predict your placements, in order. Put those pieces on the front of your rack and climb the pitch, placing your pieces as planned. Of course, if you predicted wrong, place a better piece, but this exercise is helpful for learning to look ahead and anticipate what pieces will be needed where and to develop a big-picture view of climbing safety.

Opposite: *Amelia Patterson (climbing), Eric Roed, Micah Dash, and Timmy O'Neill enjoying the social aspect of top-roping at Cannibal Crag, Red Rocks, Nevada*

CHAPTER 5

Top-Rope and Rappel Anchors

Devils Lake, Wisconsin, is made up of bullet-hard quartzite. The cliffs aren't super tall, and most routes don't offer much lead protection, so most climbers top-rope. This is a great way to start climbing or to push your limits, because falling is usually safe.

Top-roping can also be a fun way for larger groups to climb together, which is common at Devils Lake. True to friendly Midwestern values, people may even invite you onto their top rope as you hike the cliff line. On most climbs, you'll top out, see good anchors and rigging, and lower back down. Once in a while, though, you might find anchors frightful enough that you decline to lower and opt to walk back down instead. If that happens to you, or you see climbers anywhere using really poor top-rope anchor practices, politely recommend this book and/or professional instruction to the anchor builder. People don't like to be told that what they are doing is dangerous, but spreading the word about proper anchor technique is good for the sport and could prevent an accident.

This chapter covers what you need to know for building top-rope anchors using natural anchors or chocks and cams. It covers how to

- rig a slingshot top rope with the anchors on top of the cliff and the belayer on the ground below,
- set a top rope with the belayer on top of the cliff,
- protect yourself when setting anchors near the cliff's edge,
- haul your partner if they can't get up the climb,
- evaluate fixed rappel anchors,
- clean up messy anchors.

In a top-rope fall or bouncy rappel, the force on the anchors can be several times body weight, but they are not subjected to the huge forces of a leader fall unless your team makes a big mistake. Still, on every rappel and top rope, you trust your life to the system, so it's crucial to have good anchors for safety.

Once you complete a top-rope climb, you can walk off, lower down, or rappel, depending on the situation.

TOP-ROPE RACK

You don't need much gear to top-rope. If you're on a budget, forego the expensive camming units and buy hexagonal chocks and wired nuts instead. A general rack for top-roping may include the following:

- one set of wired nuts
- one set of cams or slung chocks ranging from finger- to hand-sized
- one 12- to 18-meter (40- to 60-foot) piece of either webbing or 10-millimeter-diameter or bigger climbing rope (static rope works best)
- six shoulder-length slings
- two double-length slings
- four to six carabiners
- two to four locking carabiners
- one 7- to 8-millimeter-diameter cordelette, 6 meters (20 feet) long
- one nut tool

Tailor your equipment list to meet the requirements of the area. Some top-roping areas may require different gear than what's listed above. For example, if the top anchors are bolted, you will need only a fraction of the gear listed above. Do your research before heading out.

A rack for rigging bolted top-rope stations includes the following:

- four carabiners
- four locking carabiners
- two double-length slings or four shoulder slings
- extra slings in case the bolts are not close together
- backup material if the bolts are not bomber

SLINGSHOT TOP ROPE

Probably the most common way that climbers top-rope is by using a slingshot setup: the belayer is on the ground and the rope runs up to the top anchors, then back down to the climber. This allows for good visibility and communication between the belayer and the climber, and it puts the belayer in a good position to hold the climber's weight: the carabiners at the top anchor create enough friction that the belayer feels only about 60 percent of the climber's weight, and the belayer is getting pulled up rather than down, so she can use her body weight to counterbalance the climber.

A ground anchor is generally not required when slingshot top-roping because of the friction at the top anchor. If the climber greatly outweighs the belayer, however, the belayer should be anchored to the ground. The belayer should also be anchored if she is positioned far from the spot that is directly below the anchors to keep her from getting dragged along the ground when the climber weights the rope.

If the team has constructed solid anchors and is using good belaying techniques, the biggest potential hazard probably involves rockfall. For this reason, the belayer

Warning: Do not top-rope through webbing! When lowering or falling with any slack in the system, the moving, weighted rope will cut through webbing like a knife through butter. In fact, if you need to cut webbing and don't have a knife, sawing a piece of cord back and forth across the webbing with some weight will do the job nicely.

should not be positioned directly below the climber, and especially should not be anchored beneath the climber. Rockfall is of particular concern when the climb angles such that the rope could slide across the wall with enough force to dislodge rocks if the climber falls. On all but the cleanest rock, the climber should wear a helmet, because the rope moving across the rock has a tendency to knock flakes loose from the wall above. I have seen more rockfall caused during top ropes than while following a lead, because when gear is pinning the rope to the crack or bolts, the rope's movement is limited.

A unique aspect of slingshot top-rope anchors is that the anchor will be used extensively with nobody present to monitor the anchor. For this reason, it is important to check the anchor every so often during a top-roping session. It is possible for slings and cords to wear significantly over a rough edge if repeated swinging falls are taken on a top rope.

ANCHORS AT THE CLIFF EDGE

When rigging a top rope, extend the anchors over the lip of the cliff so that the rope runs straight up, through the master point carabiners, and straight back down. If the anchors are not extended and sit above the edge, the rope must bend over the cliff edge, pass through the carabiners, and bend back over the cliff edge. This creates serious rope drag, and the rope may get damaged during the repeated falls common in top-roping if the cliff edge is even a little sharp.

PROTECTING YOURSELF WHILE RIGGING

It can be dangerous setting anchors at the edge of the cliff—one slip and it's all over. To safeguard this process, build a good anchor back from the edge of the cliff and fix a rope to this anchor. Use the fixed rope to protect yourself while you rig the top-rope anchor. Attach to the fixed rope with a prusik or clove hitch, so you can easily adjust the extension to keep yourself tight to the anchors.

prusik

The clove hitch is a bomber way to attach to the fixed rope, and it is only slightly less convenient to adjust than the prusik.

A prusik attached to a fixed line allows you to safely rig anchors at the edge of the cliff. It's wise to also tie in to the fixed rope to back up the prusik.

It's convenient to set anchors near the edge of the cliff when possible to minimize extending them. Some areas are equipped with bolts for building top-rope anchors, which makes rigging easy. Other times you may find cracks or other anchor possibilities at the edge of the cliff. Either way, two good bolts or three solid anchors, rigged to ERNEST standards, will make a good top-rope anchor. Sometimes a huge tree or giant boulder may be used as the sole anchor; the team needs to make a good judgment call on whether this is adequate.

Two-bolt top-rope anchor:

If you have bolts, you can quickly set up a pre-equalized anchor for top-roping.

Two shoulder-length slings rigged with the sliding X makes a redundant anchor with no super tight knots to untie when you're done.

The standard equalized and pre-equalized riggings shown in chapter 1 will work great if you have two good bolts or three natural anchors close together. For more options, see the belay anchor arrangements rigged with slings or a cordelette in chapter 7; these can easily be adapted to top-roping by omitting the upward-direction anchor (if one exists) and extending the anchor over the cliff edge.

ANCHORS EXTENDED OVER THE EDGE

Often you can't find good anchors at the cliff edge, or it may be an inconvenient place to rig. In these cases, you can set the anchors back from the edge and extend them to drop the master point over the lip. Always use at least two separate sets of sling, cord, or rope to extend over the lip for redundancy and pad any sharp edges with a small patch of carpet, a pack, or even a T-shirt.

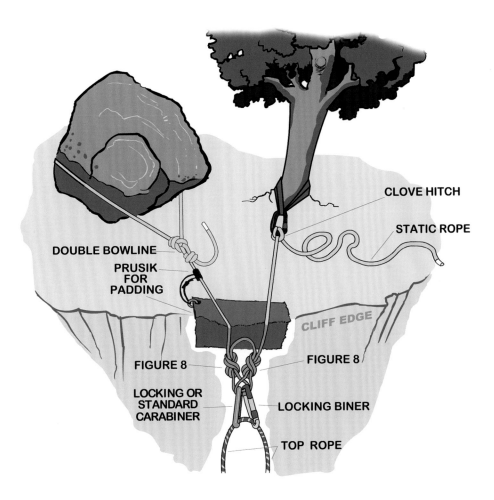

CLOVE HITCH

STATIC ROPE

DOUBLE BOWLINE

PRUSIK
FOR
PADDING

CLIFF EDGE

FIGURE 8

FIGURE 8

LOCKING OR
STANDARD
CARABINER

LOCKING BINER

TOP ROPE

Many options exist for extending the anchors past the cliff edge. This method uses a piece of 10-millimeter-diameter static rope. The rigging rope is tied around a large boulder with a double bowline and extended over the lip, where a master point is created by tying a figure eight on a bight. A second master point is tied right next to the first one for redundancy, then the rope runs back to the second anchor, a large tree, which is fixed with a sling. The rigging rope is tied to the sling with a clove hitch, and the clove hitch is adjusted so both anchors help hold the load. Finally, an old patch of carpet pads the edge and is held in place by a prusik attached to the rigging rope.

TOP BELAY

Acadia National Park has some beautiful, popular sea cliffs that are climbed mostly on top rope. The belayer anchors on top of the cliff, and the climber rappels or lowers down to a ledge just above the waterline, then gets a top rope as she climbs back out. The ambiance of the ocean and the seabirds makes the climbing seem even better than it is.

In a place like Acadia, where the bottom of the cliff is inaccessible but it's easy to get to the top, it makes sense to belay from the top. A top belay might also be used if rockfall makes belaying from the ground dangerous, or if the team is only climbing on the last pitch of a tall cliff. It can also come in handy if the cliff is taller than half a rope length and the team has only one rope. (A better option may be to tie two ropes together and use the slingshot system.) The top belay may put all of the climber's weight on the belayer and make communication difficult, so the slingshot system is usually preferable.

With a top belay, the climber is often lowered down the cliff and then climbs back up. If lowering could possibly damage the rope, or if it might be difficult for the climber to communicate when it's time to stop being lowered, the climber can also rappel, then be belayed back up on the rappel line if a good ledge or anchors

ADVANCED TIP—HAULING WITH AN ASSISTED-BRAKING BELAY DEVICE

When using an assisted-braking belay device, you can easily create a Z-pulley system to haul your partner's sorry bones up the route if he cannot climb it. Theoretically, the Z-pulley creates a 3:1 mechanical advantage, though with friction it might be more like 2:1 when using an assisted-braking device for the pulley.

Set a prusik or other friction hitch on the rope going down to the climber and clip the brake strand to this friction hitch. Configure the rope to make a Z shape (the Z-pulley system), and pull on the brake strand. Once the friction hitch touches the belay device or becomes too awkward to pull, slide it back down the rope and haul again. If the pull is too difficult, try redirecting the rope through the anchor and back to a Munter hitch on a carabiner attached to the harness—then pull down with body weight.

prusik

Opposite: *When safe and practical, rig the belay anchor so the belayer can see the climber.*

autoblock

to climber

A great system for the direct lower is to use a standard belay device attached to the anchors as shown.

A. Redirect the rope through a high carabiner (attached to the "top shelf" here) to create the necessary bend across the belay device and to add friction; finish the setup with an autoblock hitch attached to the belayer's harness to provide backup for the belayer. This method does not work well for belaying the climber up, so it is only useful if you do not plan to belay the climber back up after lowering. Note: Belayer tie-in point not shown for clarity.

B. If the climber plans to climb back up after being lowered, it is better to belay with the device on the waist and redirect through the anchor. Again, use an autoblock to back up the lower with the knot on the harness leg loops, as done when rappelling.

C. Belaying directly off the anchors with an assisted-braking belay device makes it easy to hold a fall. You need to understand the manufacturer's instructions for using these devices and make sure that the locking cam is free to move (not jammed against the wall) so it can arrest the rope.

exist for the transition from rappelling to climbing. An even safer option is to rappel on one rope while being belayed on another, then to climb with protection from the belay rope. Logistics must be well planned and communicated between the climbers to avoid problems.

RAPPEL ANCHORS

So you've topped out on *Time Wave Zero* (5.12b or 5.10 A1) in El Potrero Chico, Mexico. Now it's time to get down via the twenty-three rappels. Fortunately, the anchors are well bolted, with spare bolts for clipping the team comfortably into each rappel station. Having a good system for efficient rappelling can save hours on such a descent.

On any established rappel descent, rappel anchors are fixed in place. The anchors serve two purposes: the climbing team clips them for protection when they arrive at the station, and then they use them to anchor their rappel rope(s) for the next rappel.

Fortunately, beefy, well-designed rappel stations are becoming prevalent, although

Fixed steel rings are free to turn, so wear is not concentrated in a single point, which increases their useful life. However, be aware that horizontally spaced anchors, as shown here, are prone to twisting the rope as you belay or lower a climber.

Some climbers might worry that this arrangement has only one ring, but since the welded steel ring is probably stronger than the climbing rope, it's perfectly acceptable.

Steel chain with a diameter of 8–10 millimeters (⁵/₁₆–³/₈ inch) works nicely for feeding a rope through. Ideally the climbers who installed the hardware would have painted the chain (and bolts) camouflage, and cut the chain sections short so that they would not be an eyesore.

RAPPEL RINGS

Metal rappel rings create a low-friction path for the rope to run through when pulling for retrieval, and they cannot be melted (like a sling can be) by having a rope pulled through.

A. *Bomber. The Metolius Enviro Rap Hanger makes a bomber attachment for anchoring or rappelling; a standard bolt hanger is not a safe rappel ring.*

B. *Okay. The 6-millimeter-diameter (¼-inch) aluminum rings are intended for one-time use in mountaineering settings. It's wise to check these for wear and to back them up.*

C. *Bomber. The Fixe hanger and ring combo with a 10-millimeter-diameter (³/8-inch) welded steel ring.*

D. *Bomber. A 10-millimeter-diameter (³/8-inch) rapid link can be opened for bolt maintenance.*

E. *Good. An 8-millimeter-diameter (⁵/16-inch) rapid link also makes a good removable link or rappel ring, and it's lighter than the 10-millimeter model. Some climbers routinely carry a couple of these for rerigging rappels.*

F. *Okay. The 6-millimeter-diameter (¼-inch) rapid link is okay for one-time use but not great for permanent fixed hardware.*

G. *Bomber. A 10-millimeter-diameter (³/8-inch) lap link makes a cheap, strong rappel ring.*

H. *Bomber. You can always use a locking carabiner as a rappel ring or two carabiners with gates opposed as shown here.*

I. *Okay. In a pinch, you can use a regular carabiner with the gate taped shut as a rappel ring.*

you can still find plenty of chossy old rappel anchors. It's up to the climbing team to decide if the anchors and rigging are adequate and to rebuild or rerig if necessary. All climbers have a stake in the condition of anchors, so we also have a duty to replace or improve poor anchor setups. Some of the tattered rappel stations that still exist (usually in alpine or low-use areas) are pretty low rent and could definitely use a makeover. Sacrificing some time and gear beats risking your life on sketchy rappel anchors, and it helps prevent horrifying "I wonder if the anchors are gonna hold?" rappels. Even leaving a brand-new cam is cheap compared to the consequences of anchor failure.

BOLTED RAPPEL ANCHORS

Two or more good bolts in solid rock make a strong, convenient anchor for rappelling. The bolts also need to be fixed with rings or links for passing the rope through. Older stations may have webbing or cord fixing the rappel ring(s) to the anchors. This is okay if the material is relatively new and in good condition, but the webbing or cord looks trashy and weakens as the nylon material breaks down with exposure to the elements and ultraviolet radiation. A much better setup has rings fixed directly to the bolt hangers, with no webbing or cord involved.

A stout, well-rooted living tree can make a strong, convenient rappel anchor. Be sure to assess the quality of the tree—it is not uncommon to see dead, rotting trees with rappel slings left on them (it is possible the tree was alive and strong when the anchor was first used). Simply tie two wraps of webbing around the tree, ideally fixed with two rapid links or rappel rings. If the tree is burly enough, you can fix the slings above a branch for a convenient, high location. Smaller trees should be slung near the ground, where the sling creates less leverage, and beware of trees that are growing behind (and pressing against) flakes or unstable rock. If the tree has no slings on it, rig your own—do not wrap the rope around the tree for a rappel anchor. Although the rope can pull around the tree, the friction of the rope wears through the bark and life-sustaining cambium layer and can kill the tree.

Piton, Chock, and Natural Rappel Anchors

A large, solid rock tunnel fixed with slings and rappel rings, also called a "thread," makes a good, easy-to-rig rappel anchor. Whenever you encounter threads or slung trees with fixed slings in place, be sure to assess the full length of the slings. Sometimes rodents will chew on fixed webbing, and rockfall can easily damage the webbing on the uphill side of a tree, making the damage invisible from below. If in doubt, back it up.

When rappelling off a rock horn, make sure the horn has a good positive lip for holding the slings, and be careful to load the anchor in a downward direction when beginning the rappel. This rock horn doesn't look very secure; I'd rather find another way down.

If the anchor is worn or uses only a single aluminum rappel ring, you can quickly add two extra pieces of cord to back up the single sling and the rappel ring. It's good to carry a small knife and some cord or webbing for such operations.

A RURP, a copperhead, and a piton rigged with tattered cord, faded webbing, and a single aluminum rappel ring. Don't settle for bad rappel anchors like this.

This anchor is bad all around. It depends on a single flake, and it's rigged in the old-school American Triangle, which amplifies forces on the pieces. The V-angle in the sling is close to 90 degrees, and the sling is tied in a fashion that eliminates redundancy. Additionally, the rope runs directly through the cord, which isn't as dangerous for rappelling as it is for lowering, but pulling the rope ruins the anchor cord.

This is the same flake as in the previous photo, with a couple of improvements. If the flake is solid, this is a good rappel anchor because the nut adds a needed backup to the pitons, which are difficult to evaluate, and the carabiner ensures the anchor cord isn't compromised each time a rope is pulled through it.

You can set extra pieces to back up the rappel anchors to be cleaned by the last person down. Be sure the fixed anchor receives all of the load and bounce test it with a backup in place.

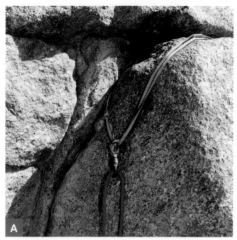 

A. In theory, the heaviest climber and gear should go first, and then the lightest climber should clean the backup pieces before descending, because he is least likely to make the anchors fail.

B. If the rappel anchors are sketchy, leave the backup in for the last person, too. The gear will be sacrificed for a good cause; the consequence of rappel-anchor failure is usually death.

EXERCISE—TOP-ROPE SCHOOL

Spend a day top-rope climbing and practice different methods for rigging and belaying the top rope. Set up and climb on the following systems:

- a slingshot top rope with natural anchors
- a slingshot top rope with cams and chocks
- a top rope with the belayer on top of the cliff

Also, practice using a self-protection system while setting anchors near the cliff edge.

Opposite: *Gerald Zauner and Guido Klingenberg airing it out on* Mingus *(8a or 5.13b), Verdon Gorge, France*

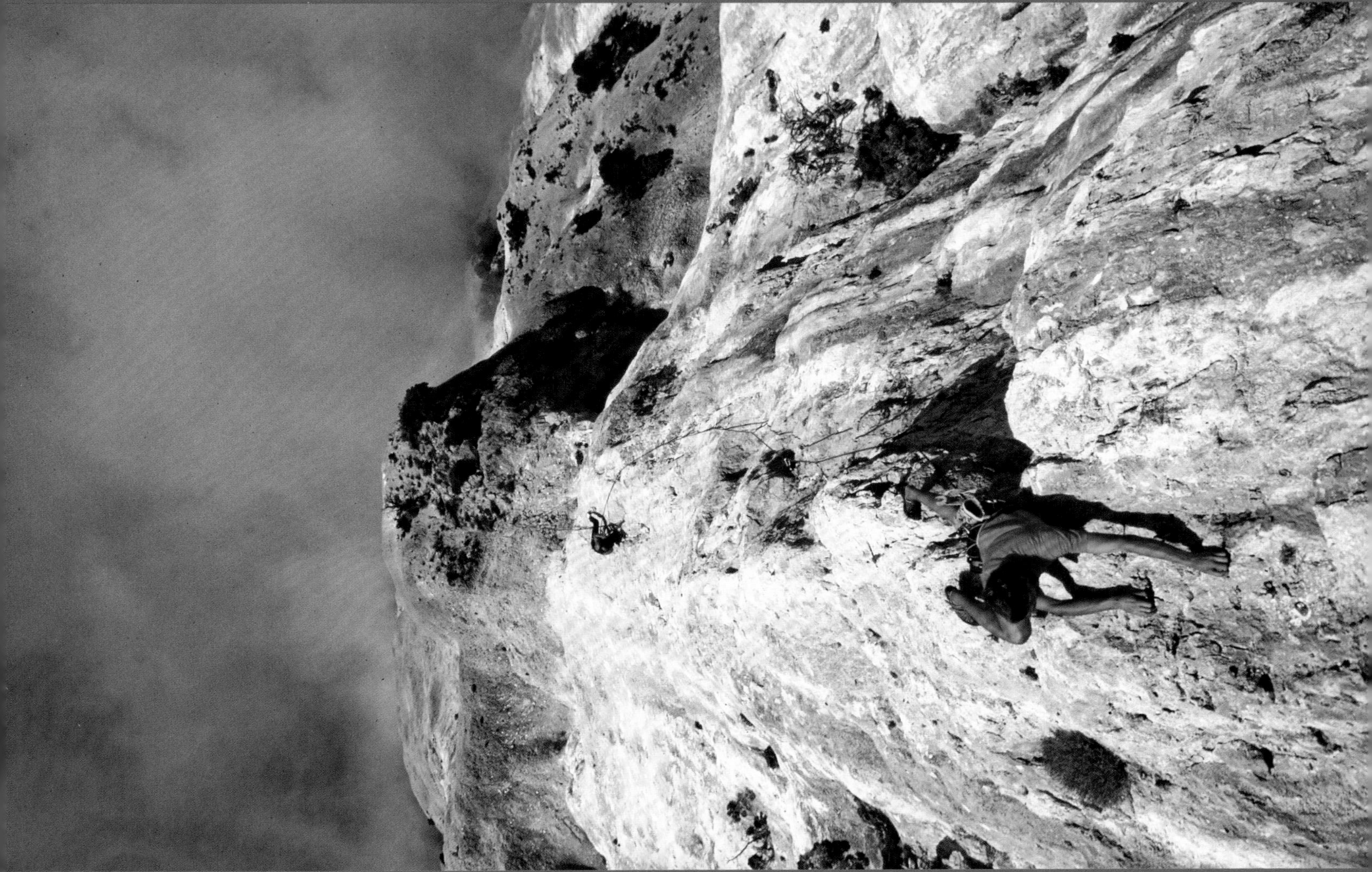

CHAPTER 6

Sport Climbing and Bolted Anchors

Smith Rock, Oregon, lies in a beautiful gorge cut by the Crooked River. During the birth of sport climbing in America during the mid- to late 1980s, the highly featured volcanic rock was bolted to create a wealth of cutting-edge sport routes. Many of the country's first 5.13 and 5.14 routes were climbed here, partly because Smith Rock was one of the first places where bolts proliferated.

Not all the routes at Smith are hard. You can find 5.7s a few dozen feet from 5.14s, with an abundance of everything in between. Some of the early bolted routes are spicy—the bolts are spaced a little farther apart than on most modern sport routes. Generally, though, it's like any sport climbing area: with preplaced bolts and little gear to carry, you can focus on the climbing. Because of the soft rock, some of the bolts are glue-ins, while others are standard mechanical bolts.

You welcome the sunshine that warms the rock as you check your knot and harness, the belayer's harness and belay device, and the stopper knot in the end of the rope. You make sure that you have enough quickdraws, all clipped in the same direction, with the rope carabiner (the one fixed in the quickdraw, often with a bent gate) hanging on the bottom. You also carry a couple slings and extra carabiners for attaching yourself to the top anchors, so you can rig the rope to lower at the top. Once you're certain that everything is in line, you start up the pitch, enjoying the feel of the rock on your fingertips.

The task of setting anchors and protection is simplified when sport climbing because the bolted anchors are already in place, waiting to be clipped.

This chapter tells you what to carry and gives a few considerations for clipping bolts, such as how to

- align the quickdraws,
- avoid dangerous carabiner orientations,
- rig anchors for lowering and top-roping,
- set up bolted belay stations for multi-pitch routes.

SPORT CLIMBING RACK

For single-pitch sport routes, you need only enough quickdraws to clip all the bolts, plus two for the top anchors and one or two spares in case you drop one. Many climbers add a couple slings with locking carabiners for the transition from climbing to lowering. A typical sport climbing rack might include the following:

- ten to fifteen quickdraws
- two shoulder-length slings
- two to three extra carabiners
- two to three locking carabiners
- one belay device

You'll need some extra gear for arranging the belay anchors on multipitch sport routes. Add the following:

- two double-length slings for rigging belay stations
- two standard carabiners
- four locking carabiners
- two belay/rappel devices with locking carabiners

If the belay stations have more than two bolts, or if you plan to set gear to back up the belays, substitute a cordelette for the double slings. It's also a good idea to carry a small knife on multipitch routes in case you have a stuck rope or need to cut cord. Multipitch sport climbs can be quite adventurous. Carrying a light set of chocks and two or three cams allows the climbers to be less at the mercy of the bolting job; a piece of trad

The standard sport climbing rack is light and simple, allowing you to focus on the climbing.

gear can eliminate a scary runout, serve as backup to a dubious-looking bolt, and save the day for rigging rappel anchors in case things don't go as planned—such as getting off-route on the descent or when a damaged rope forces shorter rappels.

CLIPPING BOLTS

Ideally, the rope runs as straight as possible as you lead a route, because each bend in the rope adds drag. If the bolts lie in a fairly straight line, short quickdraws work fine. If the bolts wander or the route climbs overhanging rock, longer quickdraws help the rope run clean. If a bolt is way off to the side or far under a roof, a shoulder-length sling might provide enough extension to keep the rope running straight.

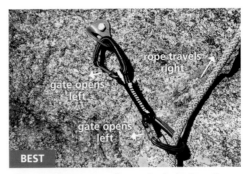

If the pitch traverses above the bolt, face the quickdraw so both gates open away from the direction of travel.

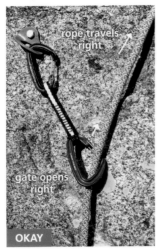

If the carabiner gate faces the direction of travel, it has a greater chance of unclipping during a fall. However, accidental unclipping is extremely rare. If other bolts provide backup, clipping this way is acceptable.

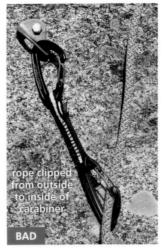

Avoid back-clipping the quickdraw, where the rope passes through the carabiner from the front and emerges on the rock side. A proper clip has the rope running from behind the biner, out the front, and to the climber without twisting the quickdraw.

Back-clipping increases the chance that the rope will accidentally unclip if you fall.

RIGGING BOLTED ANCHORS FOR LOWERING AND TOP-ROPING

At busy climbing areas, it's often best to lower back to the ground through your own carabiners to save wear on the fixed rings. The last climber down, however, will usually lower from the fixed hardware. The rope should pass through steel rings or chain links attached to at least two bolts. Most bolt hangers are sharp on the inside, and they are not intended for passing the rope directly through. Large, thick, rounded Metolius rap hangers are the exception. Sometimes the last climber down rappels rather than lowering, to save wear on the fixed rings and the rope. Before the climber begins climbing, he and the belayer should discuss whether the climber is going to lower or rappel from the top. Do not lower with the rope running through webbing!

This is a standard setup for lowering back to the ground and top-roping off a bolted anchor. Utilizing one quickdraw per bolt, face the carabiner gates out so the carabiners don't interfere with each other's gates.

DANGER

You can't be mindless about your anchors, even when sport climbing. The leader downclimbed this pitch rather than being lowered from these rusty seaside bolts. The most dangerous forms of corrosion are invisible.

DANGEROUS CARABINER ORIENTATIONS

Carabiners are strongest when loaded along their spine with the gate closed. If the gate gets pushed open, the carabiner loses about half its strength. The UIAA certification for carabiners requires open-gate and cross-loaded strength of at least 7 kN (over 1,574 pounds) of force—plenty strong enough to hold the typical sport climbing fall. If the carabiner gets leveraged over an edge, however, it can break from as little as 2.5 kN (560 pounds) of force—even a small climber generates this much force in a typical climbing fall. Pay attention to avoid dangerous carabiner orientations. Beware of excessive wear on fixed quickdraws. The rope-end carabiner can wear to a razor-sharp edge and cut a rope.

DANGER

Avoid any orientation that allows the rock to push the carabiner gate open. If the gate opens during a fall, the carabiner can lose around two-thirds or more of its strength. Carabiners are marked with their full strength, gate-open strength, and cross-loaded strength.

DANGER

A carabiner loaded over an edge could break in an average leader fall. A longer quickdraw would avoid this problem.

DANGER

This cross-loaded carabiner is sacrificing much of its strength. Pay special attention to make sure that carabiners get loaded along their spines.

A quickdraw with locking carabiners on both ends makes it impossible for the rope to accidentally unclip from critical bolts. This isn't a bad idea when accidental unclipping will result in injury, for example, when clipping the first bolts of a climb, or when climbing above a ledge. Innovative designs have produced lighter-weight locking carabiners, such as the Slider shown here at left, that, with practice, are almost as easy and fast to clip and unclip as a nonlocking carabiner. You can also use two quickdraws on a bolt if the hanger is big enough. Clip the longer quickdraw on the outside of the hanger (farthest from the rock) so that it does not get loaded unless a malfunction occurs with the quickdraw that lies closest to the rock. This technique would be used only when you're relying heavily on a single bolt.

DANGER

This kind of razor-sharp edge caused by rope wear on fixed carabiners can slice a rope like butter.

DANGER

The bolt-end carabiner can wear against the bolt hanger until the strength of the carabiner is compromised.

New technologies, such as the Bulletproof bent gate, integrate a steel insert at the point where the rope or bolt hanger makes contact with the carabiner to prevent the sharp edge of bolt hanger or the friction of the rope from wearing the softer aluminum of the carabiner.

Clipping to the bolts with the equalizer creates an anchor that splits the load equally between the bolts, even if the loading direction changes.

MULTIPITCH BOLTED ANCHORS

On multipitch sport routes, you often see climbers with bizarre rigging at the belays. Using a simple pre-equalized setup minimizes the gear required and increases the security of the rigging. If the positioning of the belay bolts is consistent from pitch to pitch, you can keep the sling tied and just clip it into each new set of anchors.

When anchors are built from modern, half-inch stainless-steel bolts, equalizing the bolts is not necessary. On hanging belays, this is an advantage because the belayer can stay suspended below one bolt, taking advantage of a foot ledge or staying out of the leader's way. A single power point in this scenario becomes awkward and inefficient.

Pre-equalizing a double-length sling to build an anchor is simple, fast, secure, and uses little gear. Here, the leader clipped one of the bolts as a first piece of protection.

This setup wastes quickdraws, and the belayer needs to take care that the quickdraws do not unclip from each other every time he weights the anchors because of the carabiner-to-carabiner attachment. No climbing accident has ever occurred from this scenario, but if a leader is climbing off of this anchor, there are better ways to clip in. For temporary bomber attachment while cleaning or threading a sport climbing anchor, enchaining quickdraws as shown is perfectly safe.

EXERCISE—SPORT ANCHORS

Beginning Sport Leaders: Hang a quickdraw, get out your climbing rope, and practice clipping until you can do it smoothly and quickly every time. Practice with right and left hands and with the gate opening right and left. Clipping well can save a few moments of fear for the leader and the belayer on those first leads.

Intermediate Sport Leaders Aspiring to Multipitch Routes: Find two bolts close to-gether or set two hangers into a piece of plywood. Clip both bolts with a double-length sling, pull two loops in the direction of loading, and tie the sling off to pre-equalize it. Now tie yourself in with a clove hitch or figure eight on a bight. Practice until you can rig the anchor in a few seconds.

Opposite: *Patience Gribble and Jason Schultz on* Energy Crisis *(5.11c), The Bugaboos, Canada*

CHAPTER 7

Traditional Belay Anchors

You awake to the familiar smell of pine, instantly aware that you're in Yosemite Valley. The route for today is the fifteen-pitch *Royal Arches*. Most of the climbing is easy, but to make good time you need to set belays fast and make quick transitions at those belays. You carry a good rack of wired nuts, hexes, and cams, along with webbing, cordelettes, quickdraws, and extra carabiners for rigging anchors.

The cracks are clean from the feet and hands of thousands of passing climbers, and the rock is solid and the anchors bomber. At each belay ledge, you custom design the anchor, trying to be quick and keep the rigging clean. Trees make a quick anchor at some of the belays, while a combination of nuts, hexes, and cams—placed in old piton-scarred cracks—works at the other stations. Whenever possible, you save the cams for the next leader by using nuts, hexes, and natural anchors at the belay.

Usually, you set at least three bomber pieces for a belay anchor. In some situations, one of the three is oriented to hold an upward pull, especially on pitches where the heavier climber is leading; or you might adjust the anchor for a sideways pull on the traversing pitches. When the three placements are small, you set more. You know how to use far more than three placements in an anchor if the placements are less than ideal, but on a trad route like *Royal Arches*, you know there is no excuse for using anything other than bomber placements in a belay; at one point you downclimb 30 feet of easy terrain to a good crack rather than belay at a flared crack where the protection options are not inspiring. When the next protection is close to the belay, and two bomber multidirectional placements are available, you build belay anchors out of only two pieces or even use just one stout tree.

Whether you're playing at your local crag or climbing the long free classics of Yosemite, being able to quickly set a variety of simple, solid belay anchors is critically important. Practice using the different anchor-rigging methods shown in this book on shorter climbs so that when you get onto longer climbs, where time is of the essence and you're trying to stretch your equipment as far as it can go, you have a range of tools at your disposal.

This chapter covers

- choosing where to belay,
- rigging belays with a cordelette,
- rigging with slings,
- rigging with the climbing rope,
- rigging with a daisy chain,
- rigging with two ropes,
- equalizing the load,
- building upward-direction anchors,
- creating multidirectional anchors,
- utilizing widely spaced anchors,
- rigging to a tree growing back from the cliff line,
- extending from the anchor so you can see and communicate with your partner.

Chapter 1 showed how to rig two- and three-point anchors with slings or a cordelette and discussed many important considerations of anchoring. Before you read on, it may be worthwhile to review the discussion in chapter 1 of pre-equalized and self-equalizing anchor-rigging systems, as well as its coverage of equalization and V-angle.

A variety of methods for rigging three- and four-piece belay anchors are shown in chapter 1. It's almost silly how many different options you have for creating a belay anchor—there's no exclusive "best way" that fits all situations. What you want is a belay anchor that's strong, simple, and fast.

BELAY STATION

Usually the standard belay stances that most teams use are marked on the topo or described in the guidebook. You don't *have* to use the described belays: if you're climbing with a new climber, it might be wise to shorten the pitches to facilitate communication and minimize rope stretch in a fall; if you're low on gear, you also might stop short; if you're trying to climb fast, you may blow past the standard belay to link up another pitch (or several pitches).

When the rock is solid and the crack splits a large, clean wall (not cracked or detached on either side), you can set the anchors close together. When the rock is fractured or otherwise suspect, however, spread the anchors out to enlist multiple rock features. Never set all the anchors behind a single detached or fractured block or flake. Set the anchors high if possible so that the master point hangs at chest-to-head level.

CHOOSING YOUR BELAY STATION

A first-rate belay station offers

- fixed anchors or good cracks for building anchors,
- safe positioning from rockfall,
- a nice ledge for comfort and stacking rope,
- sight of the climber,
- a position that minimizes rope drag for the prior pitch and the next.

You don't always get all of these qualities in a belay station. Foremost you want solid anchors and safe positioning. If you can't find good anchors or a good stance, maybe you can climb higher or even downclimb to find them. It's good for the belayer to sound the warning "Ten meters!" (or "Thirty feet!"), when that much rope remains, so the leader can start looking for a suitable belay. Once you find a good station, look around before setting the anchors. Avoid tunnel vision that focuses you on one solution only, unless that solution quickly meets all your needs.

BELAY RIGGING METHODS

As discussed in chapter 1, two good bolts or three bomber natural placements make a good belay anchor. Having great individual pieces is the most critical aspect of building a reliable belay anchor.

The time-tested recipe for a natural anchor consists of two pieces that will hold a downward pull and one piece that will hold an upward pull. If the pieces aren't great and you can't find better ones, set more and equalize them—a four- or five-point anchor is not unreasonable if the pieces are small or mediocre. If you frequently find yourself belaying on less than perfect placements, hire a guide to help. Ninety-nine percent of belays have excellent protection placements available, so there is little excuse for belaying on poor placements. You can add an upward-pull piece to protect the anchors or belayer from getting pulled up if the leader takes a hard fall, and nearly all belay anchors on multipitch climbs should be able to withstand multidirectional forces. Good lead protection just above the belay can almost be considered part of the belay anchors because it protects the anchors from a severe impact if the leader falls directly onto the belay.

Before building the anchors, analyze which direction the forces will come from, both while the second climber follows the pitch and when the leader climbs above.

Giulia Luebben clipped to a belay consisting of two Big Bros—her father's invention—placed in multidirectional placements. When both pieces are bomber and multidirectional, two-piece belay anchors are perfectly acceptable; but if in doubt, place more.

If the second's rope runs straight up to the belay, the anchors will get pulled down if he falls. If the leader is leading straight above the belay with no protection, the anchors will get pulled straight down with an extreme force if she falls. If she takes a hard fall after placing good protection, the belayer will get pulled toward the first protection, and the anchors might too. If the route traverses just before or just after the belay, the anchors can get loaded with a sideways pull. Build the anchor to be strong in any conceivable direction of pull, but even stronger in the anticipated direction of pull.

Many options exist for rigging a belay anchor. The best method often depends on the team's climbing system and the number of climbers; sometimes it's dictated by what gear is left over at the end of the pitch; at other times it's a matter of personal preference.

If most of the rack is spent by the end of the pitch, you may have to settle for a belay anchor that's less bomber than you want. You can add your body into the belay as shown in chapter 1, and once the second arrives with the cleaned gear, you can bolster the anchors before anyone leads above.

A proliferation of bolted belays has made anchoring easier, faster, and on some climbs, safer. Make sure the bolts are at least 10 millimeters (⅜ inch) in diameter and tightly fixed. Back up the bolted belay with other pieces if you have any doubts about the bolts.

Climbers often take shortcuts—some may be justifiable and some, stupid. With experience and education, a climber develops good judgment, and shortcuts should be well thought out. High-angle rock climbing falls can create large impact forces, so you can't take too many shortcuts in the belay anchor without taking a huge risk.

The belayer is tied in to the master point while belaying a leader. The leader placed protection just above the belay to protect the anchors and the belayer from a high-force fall onto the belay. The belayer could be lifted several feet in a hard leader fall. Add an upward anchor to minimize this. Belay gloves make catching hard falls easier.

Here, the cordelette rigs four pieces set in a horizontal crack. This rigging should spread the load fairly evenly among the pieces, because the leg lengths are all similar (unless the loading direction is different than anticipated). A clove hitch tied in to the rightmost piece keeps the double fisherman's knot out of the way while rigging the cordelette.

Three wired nuts and a cam rigged with the cordelette. The cam is set in a place where it can swivel to hold an upward or sideways load, making the anchor multidirectional. The short leg going to the cam may take most of the force, which may be too weak to hold a high-force leader fall onto the belay anchors. This anchor could be stronger if it were rigged to equalize the load among the pieces better.

CORDELETTE

A cordelette has multiple uses for anchoring and self-rescue. It's fast and simple for rigging three- and four-point belay anchors. A pre-equalized cordelette creates a convenient work station at the belay, with a top shelf and master point for clipping to the anchors. These clipping points are convenient if you have more than two climbers on the team. The cordelette works whether the pieces are close together or far apart, and it easily rigs

The short leg here is clipped to two pieces equalized with a half-length sling. As long as all the pieces are good, this anchor will handle anything you can throw at it.

The equalizer rigging allows you to spread the load better among the pieces, but it's slow to rig. If any anchor fails, the other anchor on that side will prevent extension. This rigging puts 50 percent of the load on the right anchors and 50 percent on the left anchors, but it's hard to spread the load evenly among the two right or two left pieces. Clipping in to both strands of the master point with separate carabiners makes the rigging redundant. The carabiners can easily slide to adjust to the pulling direction to maintain equalization.

To rig it, follow these steps:

1. Clove-hitch the two left pieces (the double fisherman's knot was placed between these two pieces to keep it out of the way).
2. Tie the two extension-limiting knots.
3. Clove-hitch the two right anchors.
4. Adjust the limiting knots and clove hitches so they sit where you want them.

multidirectional anchors. See chapter 1 for the steps to rig a cordelette.

The cordelette rigging method is sometimes criticized because it does not spread the load equally among the pieces, especially if the loading direction changes or if one leg is short. If you have bomber anchors, equalization is not so important, because any of them should be able to hold the maximum forces possible in a rock climbing fall. But if the anchors aren't great (or you're not sure), or if the leader could

There often isn't time to create complex anchor systems on long routes, but you'll pick up skills by practicing with them.

A. This anchor looks like somebody's science project. It's slow to build, but it sure does equalize—this rigging will put roughly one-sixth of the load on each of the three left pieces, and a quarter of the load on each of the two right pieces. If one piece blows, the entire load will go onto the other side of the cordelette, though. Such complex systems don't have much place on long routes, though they can be fun for engineer types who like to tinker (and maybe not so much fun for their partners, who have to wait around).

B. To rig this, tie a figure eight on a bight with a large loop in the cordelette. Clip a carabiner inside the top of the figure-eight knot, and then wrap the loop twice through the carabiner to create three clipping loops.

C. Clip the loops in to the three left anchors to equalize the load on them and tie the two extension-limiting knots.

D. Tie another figure eight on a bight with a large loop on the right side of the cordelette. Clip a carabiner inside the top of the figure eight. Clip the loop into both pieces and then back down to the carabiner in the figure eight. This equalizes the load on these two pieces. Adjust the two extension-limiting knots, then clip in to the two master point strands with separate carabiners, as shown in the first photo, to create a redundant, equalized anchor with minimal extension.

You can rig the previous anchor much more easily with one double- and two shoulder-length slings. Triple equalize the three left pieces with a shoulder-length sling and double equalize the right two pieces. Clip the double-length sling to one of the equalized slings, tie two extension-limiting knots, and then clip the double sling into the other equalized sling. Adjust the limiting knots, put a 180-degree twist into one of the clipping loops to make the sliding X, and clip in. The sliding X makes the master point redundant, so one clipping carabiner per climber works fine. Complex rigging like this is necessary only if you need to spread the load among a bunch of mediocre pieces like these microcams.

take a high-impact fall directly onto the belay anchors, a rigging method that equalizes the load better might be safer.

When used for rigging belays, the cordelette is first tied into a loop with a flat overhand, double fisherman's, or a triple fisherman's knot. If the flat overhand is used, the tails must be at least 30 centimeters (1 foot) long.

You can rig the cordelette many different ways to bring the anchors together to a common master point. Several tricks exist for improving equalization, incorporating an upward anchor, or rigging anchors that are spread far apart. When the individual placements are truly bomber, which they should be the vast majority of the time, the more complex equalization methods shown here are not necessary. But if you find yourself in the terrifying situation of needing to rig a belay on marginal protection, knowing how to craft an equalized belay is a critical skill.

Upward-Pull Anchor Built In to Station

Upward anchors serve two purposes: to hold the belayer down and to protect the other anchors from an upward pull. When it's important to hold the belayer down, an independent upward anchor, placed below the belayer and attached to the belayer separately from the main anchor as shown in chapter 1, usually works best.

You can incorporate an upward directional placement into the rigging to create a multidirectional belay anchor that can withstand a pull in any direction. This can protect the anchors against an upward pull and limit the distance the belayer can get lifted.

The upward directional anchor should be the lowest piece.

Sometimes a cam set for a downward pull in a parallel crack is sufficient to counter the upward pull because the cam will swivel and lock to hold an outward, sideways, or upward pull. However, in "wavy" rock, the cam lobes might open up if the cam swivels; such a placement may not be reliable against an upward pull.

Horizontal cracks can provide excellent opportunities to create multidirectional anchors with only two pieces. Two bomber, equalized placements in a horizontal crack can create an ERNEST anchor with minimal equipment.

Cams in relatively parallel-sided cracks can often provide a multidirectional piece.

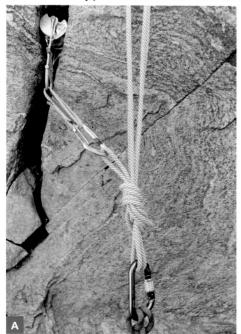

A. This anchor can handle an upward pull because the low cam will swivel to the new pulling direction. The leg going to the cam is short, so this piece may feel most of the force if the leader falls directly onto the belay. This belay anchor is good only if the other two pieces are bomber too.

B. When pulled upward, the cam swivels to confront the new pulling direction.

This rigging method cinches two opposing anchors tight against each other to actively hold the pieces in place and create a multidirectional anchor. You can also do this with a sling as shown in chapter 1.

A. Set four anchors in a crack. The lowest two should be opposing. Clip the cordelette loop in to the upward-pull anchor, and clip both cordelette strands through the lowest downward-pull anchor.

B. Pass the opposite end of the cordelette between the two strands and through the upper carabiner again.

C. Pull the cord tight to cinch the pieces against each other.

D. Clip the cordelette loop to the remaining pieces, and pull a loop down between each piece.

E. Pull all the loops in the expected direction of loading.

F. Tie the cordelette off with an overhand or figure eight to create the master point and top shelf.

ADVANCED TIP—KEEPING THE MASTER POINT HIGH

Having the master point at chest-to-head level makes a convenient work station. Here are three tricks for shortening the cordelette to keep your master point high if the anchors are close together.

Left: *This cordelette was used to clove-hitch the lowest two pieces to oppose each other, making the anchor multidirectional. The third piece from the bottom is clipped twice, which uses more cord and keeps the master point higher. The double loops may give this piece more than its share of the load because that leg won't stretch as much as the others.*

Right: *Tie another knot in the loop, farther from the ends of the cordelette, to shorten the loop and keep the master point high.*

A. *If you still have too much cord when it's time to tie off the cordelette, keep passing the cord around itself as you tie the figure eight—to create a figure nine.*

B. *The figure-nine knot uses up much of the extra length of the cordelette.*

Anchors Set Far Apart

If one of the anchors is far above the others, you have a few options for extending it down. Following are solutions for rigging the same set of anchors with a cordelette.

A. The cordelette can work for distant anchors if you untie the loop and tie a figure eight on a bight in each end. Clip one figure eight to the high anchor, the other to the low anchor, and clip the cord in to the remaining anchors. In this case, the lowest two pieces are wired nuts set in opposition to create a multidirectional placement. The nuts are clipped together with two carabiners (gates opposed) due to the three-way pull and possible cross-loading on the carabiner.

B. Pull the cord down in the direction of loading as normal and tie it off to create the master point. The extended cordelette works fine, but it does not provide a full-strength top shelf. With this rigging, the highest piece probably won't share much of the loads because the leg is so long and it's only a single strand, which will stretch more easily than the two-strand loops, but it's still there to serve as a backup.

Here, the lower anchors were rigged with a cordelette, and the climbing rope was extended to the backup anchor. The cordelette was shortened by tying a flat overhand knot to isolate some cord so the master point could be kept high.

Tying Up the Cordelette

It's important to keep the cordelette organized as you climb.

A. *Spread your fingers to form a spool. Grab the knotted side of the cordelette.*

B. *Wrap the cord repeatedly around your hand until you have a loop about 40–60 centimeters (16–24 inches) long remaining.*

C. *Wrap the remaining loop tightly around the coil. When there's only a small length of loop left, push it through the top of the coil.*

D. *Clip this loop to carry the cordelette.*

SLINGS

Advancements in webbing material have created slings that are extremely light, compact, and strong. These new materials make it convenient to rig belay anchors with slings, allowing the climbing team to dump the heavier cordelettes. Rigging with slings also makes it easier to equalize the load among the pieces.

Slings are frequently used to rig belay anchors, but often in a messy, time-consuming, gear-wasting fashion. A few nice solutions exist that are clean and efficient. The techniques shown in this chapter require only a sling or two and some carabiners for rigging three- or four-point belay anchors. When the belay will be weighted heavily even without a fall, such as a hanging belay, minimize the number of knots tied in the webbing—these can be difficult and time-consuming to untie.

Many ways exist for rigging anchors with slings. These methods are great to know in case you drop your cordelette, use it for lead protection, or see a quick and bomber alternative to the cordelette. To learn to use these methods efficiently when you need them, it's important to practice rigging with slings even when you have a cordelette available. Challenge yourself to rig at least one bomber anchor without a cordelette every time you go climbing. Many advanced climbers choose not to carry a cordelette at all in order to conserve weight and time, and any climber who aspires to multipitch efficiency should be comfortable rigging anchors with and without a cordelette.

This clean arrangement uses only a double-length sling to equalize the load between the left cam and the two pieces on the right. The two extension-limiting knots make the clipping point of the sliding X redundant, and they allow for some directional shift while limiting extension if the anchor blows. An upward-pull anchor is clipped with another sling to the master point.

To rig it, follow these steps:

1. Clove-hitch the lower-right piece.
2. Clip the upper-right piece.
3. Add the two limiting knots.
4. Clip the left piece.
5. Adjust the knots and clip in between them with a sliding X.

This is a reasonable anchor, but it's not as clean as the previous rigging. The upper two anchors are equalized with a sliding X, and an overhand knot minimizes extension if the highest piece fails. The upper two anchors are then equalized with the right anchor via a sliding X in a half-length sling (half the length of a shoulder sling to minimize extension if a piece fails). The lower clipping point is not redundant, so the rope is also clipped to the upper locking carabiner to back up the half-length sling. These placements in a horizontal crack will hold an upward pull, so no extra upward anchor is necessary.

A little slack between the clipping knots ensures that the lower carabiner gets loaded so it can equalize the force between all three pieces. As it's rigged, the two left pieces will each hold 25 percent of the force, while the right piece holds 50 percent. If the load comes onto the upper tie-in, the left two pieces will hold the entire load, and the right anchor will not contribute at all.

These four pieces are rigged with a four-loop sliding X using two double-length slings for redundancy. This rigging is fast and simple, and it equalizes the load among the four pieces, with each anchor holding around 25 percent of the load. If the loading direction changes, the slings will shift in the clipping carabiner to maintain equalization. If one piece fails, the slack disperses among the other three loops so that extension is minimal. To rig it, follow these steps:

1. Clip both slings to all four pieces.
2. Pull a loop down between each piece.
3. Put 180-degree twist in each loop.
4. Clip all four loops with a large locking carabiner.

The guide's belay. The autoblocking belay device is clipped in to the top shelf of the cordelette, while the belayer is clipped in to the master point. The two attachments can be switched for convenience and ease of use or to accommodate larger teams of climbers. This method is not safe except with an autoblocking or assisted-braking belay device.

A shoulder sling and double-length sling combine to create three fixed legs, similar to a cordelette rigging. The shoulder sling is tied off with an overhand knot to shorten it. If the rock quality is in doubt, improved equalization would be a better choice.

A double-length sling can rig a three-point anchor if two of the anchors are in line with each other. The lower-left nut clips just below a knot in the sling that eliminates the possibility of extension. The sling is pre-equalized, creating redundancy and a solid master point for the team to clip. While this method is fast and convenient for rigging bomber anchors, the first rigging with slings (shown at the beginning of the chapter) equalizes the load better.

If the belayer gets lifted, she might pull out the low nut. An upward anchor could be clipped to the nut, the master point, or directly to the belayer to prevent this.

An adjustable hitch works well to precisely adjust sling length and is easy to untie after heavy loading. In the example here, the adjustable hitch is used to rig a minimalist anchor with two pieces; the lower piece is a cam that can rotate to hold an upward pull, and both are bomber in a downward pull, meeting two-downward and one-upward minimum for a belay anchor. Ideally, a third piece would be added before the leader sets off on the next pitch. Here's how to tie an adjustable hitch:

A. Hang a sling from the upper of two pieces.

B. Tie a simple slipknot in one side of the sling with the sliding part of the knot leading toward the upper carabiner.

C. Clip the loop of the slipknot into the upper carabiner.

D. Adjust until the bottom of the sling is close to the same height as the lower piece.

E. Clip in to both the bottom of the sling and the lower piece.

F. Adjust the sliding hitch to match the lower piece as well as the anticipated direction of pull.

A double sling with a sliding X and an extension-limiting knot splits the load between the right anchor and the left two anchors. The upper-left cam is clipped in to the sling of the lower-left cam to save gear, and the pieces are positioned to share the load. A lightweight locking carabiner on the lower-left cam adds security since it connects two of the anchors to the rigging sling.

The sling is not redundant in its master point. Tying another extension-limiting knot in the sling just below the left cams would make it redundant. You could also tie the rope in to the second locking carabiner. An upward anchor can be clipped in to the master point.

The equalized lower pieces comprise the primary anchor, with the highest piece serving as a backup. By tensioning the upper clove hitch more you can get all three anchors sharing the load. This isn't perfectly equalized, but it's fast. It would be even faster if you eliminated the extension-limiting knots and used a half-length sling to equalize the left two pieces.

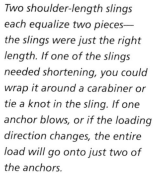

Two shoulder-length slings each equalize two pieces—the slings were just the right length. If one of the slings needed shortening, you could wrap it around a carabiner or tie a knot in the sling. If one anchor blows, or if the loading direction changes, the entire load will go onto just two of the anchors.

The top two cams are pre-equalized with a double-length sling. The knot creating the master point was adjusted so the hexagonal chock could clip in to the master point and contribute to the anchor. You can often slide the cam placements up or down to adjust the position of the sling. The hex looks like it might not handle an upward pull very well, though some crystals do hold it against an outward pull. You might add an upward anchor clipped to the master point or the belayer. This setup doesn't equalize great, but it's quick to rig and requires minimal gear.

The Darwin anchor. Climbers who set anchors like this will be removed from the gene pool. All of the pieces are set in a single detached flake, the hexes look like they could pull out easily, the rigging wastes quickdraws and carabiners, and it all relies on a single, nonredundant sling that doesn't even have a sliding X—if the left hex rips, you get total failure. To top it off, the climber is clipped in using a clove hitch and a single nonlocking carabiner. If the leader falls before setting good protection, this team is toast.

ADVANCED TIP—MULTILOOP KNOTS

You can create multiple clipping loops in the rope by tying a double-loop figure eight, a double bowline, or an equalizing figure eight. These methods use a fair amount of rope, so avoid them on rope-stretcher pitches.

The double bowline (see appendix 2) works well for clipping two anchors, such as this pair of bolts. Appendix 2 shows how to tie this knot, as well as the double-loop figure eight, which also creates two clipping loops. This belayer is clipped in to the bolts with two locking carabiners. Lightweight locking carabiners don't add much weight to the rack, but they can add some extra security at the belay, though nonlocking carabiners should be fine too.

This bolted belay is nice because it has a third bolt for the leader to clip before setting off on the pitch. The bolt would be better positioned a little higher. The belayer could also tie in to this bolt if she is concerned about the quality of her two belay bolts.

The equalizing figure eight (see appendix 2) can adjust if the loading direction changes, though it may not give perfect equalization due to friction in the knot. As shown here, collapse one of the three loops to clip only two anchors.

You can clip three anchors with the equalizing figure eight. It's best if the anchors are good, and not too far apart, so the rope can't burn across itself if an anchor fails. You can tie an extension-limiting knot in the longest loops if you're concerned about that.

By making a bigger loop in the beginning and passing it through the figure eight one extra time, you can get four or five loops for clipping. Here, four anchors are clipped, and the fifth loop is collapsed.

To create a master point, tie a figure eight on a bight in the rope just below the multiloop knot. You can belay the second directly from this master point if you have an assisted-braking belay device.

Daisy Chain or PAS

Using a daisy chain or PAS is a popular way to add both efficiency and redundancy to an anchor. The most efficient way to use a daisy in the case of two-bolt anchors is to clip one anchor with the daisy and the other with the rope. Variations on this theme work great for three-piece trad anchors as well: clip one piece with the daisy, equalize the other two, and clip them with a clove hitch in the rope.

Sometimes the cordelette wouldn't work anyway because the anchor is too funky and using a cordelette would limit the options. Here, the two pieces close together form the primary anchor, and the tree in the distance, attached with one of the double ropes, is used as a backup. Be willing to be creative.

ROPE

You can tie in to all the anchors with the climbing rope for fast anchoring that requires minimal gear. Anchoring with the

The old-school method. One of the quickest and easiest ways to get in to a series of anchors is to clip each one of them with a clove hitch. Cinch the clove hitches from bottom to top so all the anchors contribute, though it's impossible to distribute the load equally with clove hitches. This is fast when you're swinging leads, but it's hard to clip another climber in to this anchor.

rope works well for a party of two who are swinging leads; with bigger teams, or if one person is leading all the pitches, it can be awkward getting climbers clipped in and out of the anchors because no master point exists, but it can be done safely. Tying the belayer's rope up in the rigging also makes it difficult (but not impossible) to escape the belay in an emergency.

Half Ropes

If you happen to be climbing with two twin, half, or single ropes, you can tie each rope to a different anchor cluster to make a quick belay anchor.

Trees

In some areas, you can frequently tie off a tree as an anchor.

If you use the rope to rig anchors that are spaced horizontally, use the "triangle tie-in" to keep yourself tight to all the anchors. The rope runs from the belayer up to the two left anchors, where it's tied in to each with a clove hitch. Then it's tied to the right anchor with another clove hitch, and finally it runs back to the belayer's harness where it's tied with a fourth clove hitch. This rigging makes it easy to adjust the rope lengths so that all the anchors hold some of the load. The first protection was placed before the leader left the belay, so the belay essentially included four good anchors. The best clove-hitch anchor is often a combination of two equalized pieces with a third clipped as backup.

You could increase the strength of this belay anchor by equalizing the two left pieces. The lowest piece is a stopper, which probably won't hold an upward pull. An upward-pull anchor might be a good idea here, to protect the belayer and the lowest anchor from getting lifted in a leader fall.

The lowest piece is a stopper, which could get pulled out with an upward pull—an upward-pull anchor might be in order. This anchor could be strengthened by equalizing the two left anchors at the cost of a sling, carabiner, and a few seconds of time.

Wrapping the rope around a stout tree and clipping it back to your belay loop makes an anchor with only one carabiner, as a young Giulia Luebben demonstrated here. Make sure the tree isn't covered in sap. You also might want your belayer to be more than two years old.

Sometimes you want to anchor to a tree set back from the cliff's edge at the top of a route. One convenient method is to pre-equalize a cordelette around the tree and then clip your rope in with a locking carabiner and lock it. Now go back to the cliff edge and tie a clove hitch in the rope and attach it to a locking carabiner on your belay loop. Lock the carabiner and cinch the rope up tight to fasten yourself to the tree. This rigging doesn't create a master point, so the climber is belaying directly off her harness belay loop.

You might want anchors at the cliff edge to back up the tree, prevent rope stretch, or give you directional stability (if the belay position is not in line between the tree and the climber). There are many ways that you could rig this. Here, the belayer clipped the tree and went back to the cliff edge. Then she set the extra anchors, pre-equalized them, and clipped her rope in to the pre-equalized sling. Finally, she clipped the rope into her tie-in carabiner to connect the tree to the other anchors.

This climber was nearly out of rope, but she wanted to belay close to the cliff edge to reduce rope drag and to communicate with her partner. The tree is set back from the lip, so she pulled up slack and clipped the rope in to her harness belay loop with a clove hitch on a locking carabiner so she couldn't drop the rope. Then she rigged a sling around the tree, untied her original tie-in knot, and tied the rope's free end to the sling.

She belayed herself to the lip by feeding rope through the clove hitch. Then she set two pieces at the lip to back up the tree and to help keep her in position if her partner were to fall. She pre-equalized the two pieces and tied the rope in to them. Finally, she tied a figure eight on a bight to create a master point. She clipped her belay loop directly in to the master point and rigged the belay device. After she was secure, she untied the clove hitch that protected her while she rigged at the lip.

ADVANCED TIP—EXTENDING THE ANCHOR

Guides often extend themselves from their belay anchor so they can see and communicate with their clients. This is a great technique if your partner needs to be coached and the anchors are out of view of the climber.

A. Set the anchors and clip the rope in to the master point with a Munter hitch.

B. Move down to the belay spot, belaying or lowering yourself on the Munter hitch if necessary. Pull rope down to get some slack and tie an overhand in both rope strands. The overhand knot anchors you and creates a master point.

C. You can do a direct belay with an autoblocking belay device off the master point.

D. If the terrain is tricky, you can belay the whole team back to the anchors by pulling the rope through the Munter hitch.

EXERCISE—BELAY ANCHORS

Find a safe, level place where you have access to some cracks. Set several belay anchors and try rigging the same pieces with a cordelette, slings, and just the climbing rope. Use the minimal amount of gear to make a strong, redundant anchor. This doesn't mean taking shortcuts or setting sketchy anchors; it simply means rigging as cleanly and efficiently as possible. Try many of the different configurations shown in this chapter to see what works well in different situations. Use a variety of cams, nuts, and other gear, and be particularly critical of the individual placements—solid placements are the most important part of the belay anchor. If possible, have a guide or experienced climber evaluate your work.

Opposite: *Vera Schulte-Pelkum pulling plastic and eyeing the clip*

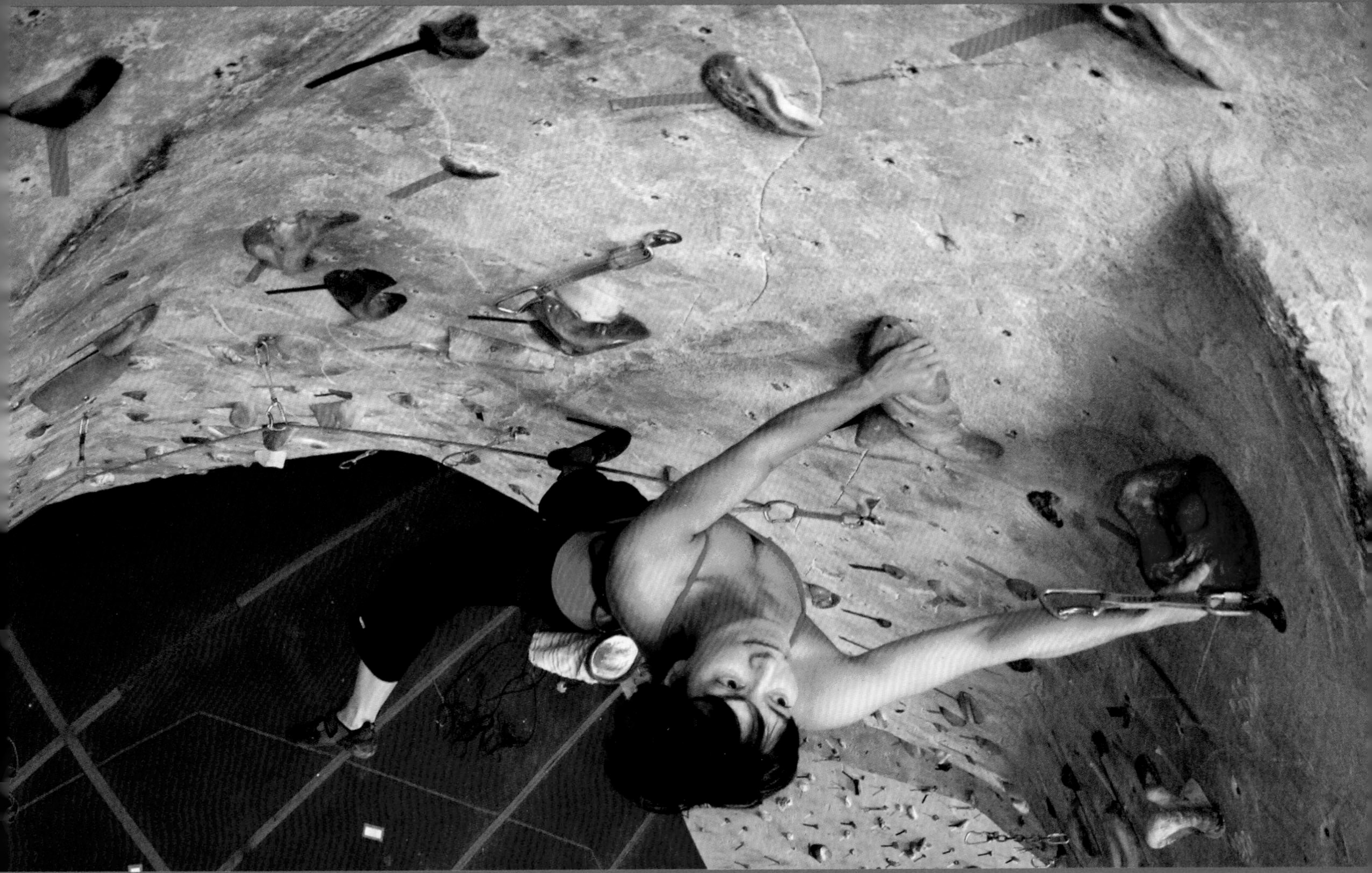

CHAPTER 8

Gym Anchors

Most climbers today are introduced to the vertical world not at some intimidating crag of wind- and water-sculpted stone, but in the friendly, seemingly safe, human-built and climate-controlled environment of the climbing gym. This evolution of the game has been an incredible boon to people all over the world and has made the sport more colorful, diverse, powerful, and accessible. No longer do you have to be lucky enough to live in a region with access to natural rock; some of the strongest climbers in the game built their first finger callouses and climbing muscles in cities far, far away from any climbable natural rock.

Additionally, climbing gyms have changed the culture of climbing, including how people are introduced to safety systems. The idea of a "belay test," still scoffed at by old-timers visiting new climbing gyms, has added a comforting standard to climbing safety. Not long ago, belaying was taught either by guides—the best source of climbing education—or by whoever happened to take you climbing for the first time, who may not have been the best source of climbing education. Today, a belay test is given to the majority of people who learn to climb, and that's a great place to start.

On top of contributing to what is arguably a change for the better in beginner belay skills, gyms have added a fantastic social element to climbing, made everyone stronger, and inspired a more dynamic style of climbing that is dictated not by the natural form of the rock, but rather by the creativity of the route setters and hold manufacturers.

However, gym climbing is far from a no-brainer and comes with its own unique hazards and anchor considerations. These include

- best practices with slingshot top ropes,
- ground anchors for belaying heavier leaders,
- auto-belay systems,
- how the bolts that are clipped influence fall trajectory and length,
- anchor strategy to optimize climbing performance.

BELAYING IN THE GYM

Why is belaying a consideration in a book about anchors? Particularly in the gym? Because climbing is a system with a climber on one end, a belayer on the other, and an anchor point in between. When compared to climbing outdoors, most gym climbing happens close to the belayer and often with bystanders milling around directly beneath the climber, where a longer than expected fall can quickly result in injury. Also, gym climbs typically have much less rope drag than outdoor climbs, where surface features almost always create some additional drag. This rope drag can be a problem, but in small doses, rope drag acts as a buffer between the belayer, anchor, and climber, allowing smaller belayers to hold bigger climbers more easily.

This is equally applicable for short, smooth climbs outdoors; anytime there is no rope drag, the belayer feels the fall force more dramatically. As long as the belayer and climber are close to the same weight—within approximately 20 percent of each other—communication is all that is needed to prevent unexpectedly long falls or slamming the belayer into the wall. Communication should include these topics:

- weight differences (yep, climbing is one place you want your partner to know your weight);
- any particular strategy, such as skipping the first bolt (not allowed in some gyms, so check);
- letting other climbers in the area know if you see an anchor position that could cause a fall trajectory onto the climber, the belayer, or a bystander.

Anytime the climber outweighs the belayer by more than about 20 percent, it is possible that the belayer could be thrown hard into the wall, the leader could fall farther than expected, or the belayer and climber could even collide in midair. To prevent these scenarios, belayer positioning, ground anchors, and/or Ohm assisted-braking resistor use should be considered.

Clipping out of the plumb line can be a good idea if the route wanders, but if you get too creative with your clipping, you may end up with heavy rope drag.

SLINGSHOT TOP-ROPE USE

The majority of gym top ropes are set up with an anchor consisting of the rope running one full wrap around a fat pipe positioned along the top of the wall. This method has two advantages: first, it is possible to slide the rope along the pipe to achieve a belay from directly overhead on a variety of routes. Second, this configuration makes it easier to hold the climber because the rope's wrap around the pipe creates more friction than simply running it over the pipe once or through carabiners or rings. Although this pipe-wrap configuration has become the standard for most modern gyms, there are still gyms where the rope only passes over the pipe or runs through rings. A good belay can be provided in any top-rope configuration—just don't be taken by surprise by less friction than you expect when the climber falls or lowers.

Just like with an auto belay, climbing to the side of the anchor point exposes the climber and others to a potentially hazardous swing. You can develop a sense of top-rope swing potential with this exercise:

1. Pick a climb without obstacles on either side, including climbers, big hold features, or walls that you could swing into.
2. Inform your belayer of your plan to swing.
3. Climb just a couple of feet to one side.
4. Jump off!

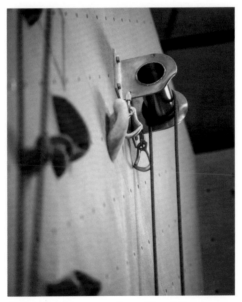

A slingshot top-rope setup with a full wrap around a belay pipe.

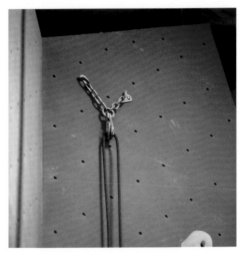

A slingshot top-rope setup with the rope running through two carabiners. This setup will provide significantly less friction than the wrapped-pipe anchor—be ready for more force than you might expect.

5. Climb to about 10 feet below the anchor and repeat the short swinging fall.

Pay attention to the difference between the two falls—as you near the anchor, you will swing much harder and faster than when you are far below the anchor—and assess your line of ascent accordingly on future climbs.

BELAYER POSITIONING

The farther the belayer stands away from the wall, the less gravity helps him catch a fall. This, like many things in climbing, is a double-edged sword. Usually, it is best to stand almost directly under the first anchor. However, while the leader is climbing near the first couple of bolts, her fall trajectory will most likely be directly onto the belayer if the belayer is standing under the first bolt. For this reason, most savvy belayers will start out a bit to one side, perhaps even changing sides if the climber moves to the other side of the line of bolts, and eventually end up directly under the first bolt.

DANGER

Do not belay too far from the wall. If the leader takes a hard fall, this belayer will be slammed into the wall with significant force and may even lose control of the belay.

The belayer should stand no more than about a body's length from the wall. (Consider trying out belay glasses, which can prevent neck strain.)

GROUND ANCHORS

Most gyms provide ground anchors but leave it up to the individual climbing teams to determine if they want to use one. Experienced smaller belayers often prefer the freedom of not using the ground anchors so that they can move around relative to the leaders, but even the most experienced belayers will be wise to use ground anchors when belaying leaders who outweigh belayers by a third or more. It's up to you and your partner to decide if a ground anchor should be used.

When using a ground anchor, it may not be possible or practical to change location relative to the first bolt, but careful evaluation of the line of ascent will help to determine where to position the ground anchor.

The most common ground anchor is a sandbag with a daisy chain attached. Clip the daisy at the length that removes slack between the belayer and the bag as shown with the red sling.

ASSISTED-BRAKING RESISTOR

As usual in climbing technology development, need results in innovation, and Edelrid's Ohm device is no exception, giving smaller belayers an excellent tool to even the playing field of body size. The Ohm is not a belay device and does not replace the belayer. The Ohm is designed to increase friction at the first bolt if the leader should fall and to reduce the force on the belayer. During a climb, the Ohm will run smoothly without causing additional friction. When used correctly, this device largely eliminates the need for a bottom anchor and gives smaller belayers added confidence and safety. Experiment with the device on a few easier climbs before using it to belay a leader on a difficult route.

AUTO-BELAY USE

Maybe one day someone will rig an auto belay with a thousand-foot tether to the top of the *Rostrum* in Yosemite, but for now auto-belay devices are exclusively used indoors. Mechanical failure of auto-belay devices is exceedingly rare, although it has happened (wheels fall off cars sometimes too). Human error is a more common culprit, and these auto-belay accidents have occurred due to two main mistakes:

Forgetting to clip in. Climbers ranging from young kids to alpine veterans have simply forgotten to clip in to the auto belay before heading up the wall, then fall from the top when they let go. You may scoff, but imagine how easy it can be to overlook something when your nerves are fried from

Here's how to use the Ohm if you are leading:
1. *Clip the device to the rope per the manufacturer's instructions and the diagram on the device, and clip the device to your harness before starting up the climb.*
2. *Instead of clipping the first quickdraw with the rope, clip the upper link or carabiner with the quickdraw that comes attached to the Ohm from the manufacturer.*
3. *Climb past the Ohm just as you would a regular quickdraw.*

Here's how to use the Ohm if you are belaying:
1. *Position yourself so the rope bends at an angle as it passes through the Ohm. It is this angle that adds friction, so belayer position is important.*
2. *Stand about a body's length to the side out from the base of the climb to create the angle that will activate the Ohm if the leader falls.*
3. *Stay ahead of the leader's clips so the device is not lifted when the leader is clipping. Even a small amount of friction caused by the belayer will be multiplied by the Ohm and make it difficult for the leader to clip quickly.*
4. *Do not stand directly under the first bolt, because this removes the angle that is needed for the device to work. In this scenario, the Ohm will not cause additional friction and will behave like a quickdraw.*

DANGER

Some gyms have reminders posted to help with the seemingly obvious step of clipping in to the auto belay, but it's a surprisingly easy step to miss.

This climber is too far to the left of the auto belay. If she falls, she will swing hard to the right, hitting the corner to her right or any other climber who happens to be in the way.

a day of work, you're fresh out of rush-hour traffic, only have an hour free to climb, and you're moving quickly from one auto belay to another with your earbuds rockin' and no partner to keep an eye on you.

Climbing too far to one side. Every foot you deviate to one side of the plumb line below the auto belay is nearly 2 feet of swing. This means if you're 5 feet to the left of the device, you're going to swing nearly 10 feet, most of it carrying quite a bit of momentum and potential force if you hit either another wall, a feature on

the wall, or—worst of all—another climber. Limit your route to the holds within a few feet to the left or right of the line where the webbing from the auto-belay anchor was hanging before you clipped in.

LEAD ANCHORS

The lead anchors in climbing gyms are closely spaced, strong, professionally maintained, and easy to understand and use safely. However, just like any lead climbing,

DANGER

Even in the safe setting of the gym, dangers exist. This climber is too far to the left of her line of bolts, and if she falls, she will slam into the wall to the right and, to make matters worse, may even hit the protruding red holds.

it is important to develop a keen sense of potential consequences, and because the climbs in a gym can be so close to each other, you can pose a risk to other climbers, and other climbers can pose a risk to you.

FALLING

Gravity works exactly the same indoors as it does outdoors, but there are a few considerations for falling in the gym that are unique to indoor climbing and gym anchors. These include lack of rope drag, other climbers

close by, potential confusion about which bolts or anchors to clip, and clipping holds.

WHICH BOLT TO CLIP?

Many modern gyms are grid-bolted to geometric perfection. This way, the route setters need to focus only on the holds and the movement and can leave the bolts and quickdraws in place without changing them to fit a new route. Although this adds an element of confusion to the climbing experience, it also affords the leader some flexibility to choose which bolts to clip, depending on a variety of factors:

- Shorter climbers can often clip different bolts than taller climbers.
- When another leader is climbing nearby, clipping a bolt away from the other leader can prevent a leader fall that could hit the other climber.
- The climber can clip from the best holds.
- The climber can clip bolts that avoid dangerous swings into features or other climbers.

CLIPPING AND SAFETY

As mentioned earlier, there is usually very little rope drag on gym routes, and even if there is drag created by the rope running over an edge, around a feature, or through a zigzag of clips, the climbs are not long enough for the drag to become a problem. Thanks to having so many bolts, the potential fall length in the gym is kept fairly short; there is, however, one dramatic exception: falling off with an armload of rope while clipping. Even for experienced climbers, it is difficult to anticipate how

With the last bolt at waist level, this climber went from risking a 10-inch fall to a nearly 10-foot fall because she pulled up rope to clip from too low. If her hand is on a good hold, this might be okay, but if she is tired and the hold is meager, it is possible to fall with an armload of slack and take a dangerously long fall.

It might be safer to climb higher to a better hold before clipping.

much the armload of rope will add to the length of a fall.

It doesn't take many leads to learn that it is best to avoid falling off while clipping. Preventing this takes a combination of boldness, discipline, and planning. The trad master may laugh at the concept of boldness in the gym, but it is often best to climb

a bit higher before clipping to avoid pulling up as much slack to make the clip. Many gym climbers prefer to clip with the bolt just a little above the waist rather than clipping from far below. Consider the following when deciding where to clip:

- Look ahead at the next holds to see if one of them might be a better clipping hold.
- Adjust foot position to optimize stability and reduce strain on the arms as much as possible.
- Visualize the clip to determine which hand to clip from—sometimes it is best

This bolt is clipped correctly, with the leader side of the rope on the outside of the carabiner.

This bolt is clipped incorrectly, with the leader side of the rope passing behind the gate of the carabiner. In this case, when the leader falls, the rope will pass across the gate and may unclip as shown in the image to the right.

to reach across and clip with the hand farthest from the bolt.

- Be particularly careful at the second through fourth bolts—falling with an armload of slack while close to the ground can cause the leader to hit the ground, the belayer, or a bystander.

When clipping, you want the rope to run so that it passes between the carabiner and wall and then out to the climber. This subtle difference is tricky for new leaders to grasp at first, but ask yourself this question to see if you have clipped correctly: When I move above this anchor, will the rope *cross* the gate of the carabiner? This prevents the dangerous scenario where the rope can, in the case of a fall, drop across the gate of the carabiner and possibly come unclipped.

TOP ANCHORS

There are a variety of top anchors found in climbing gyms, but the most common is simply two quickdraws hanging next to each other. Be sure to clip the anchor so the rope is not pinched between the two carabiners or you may find your rope locks when you try to lower, and being rescued in the gym, while safer for the rescuers, is even more embarrassing than being rescued outside.

ANCHORS AND PERFORMANCE

There is a baseline standard for using gym anchors safely, and this isn't difficult to achieve, provided the leader and belayer both pay attention and understand the fundamentals, but using anchors to optimize performance and enjoyment is a little more complex. It's worth adding anchor use to your performance plan, however, because using the anchors well makes hard climbing more fun.

CLIPPING TECHNIQUE AND PERFORMANCE

Nobody likes fumbling with a clip. It detracts from the climbing, is sometimes scary, saps confidence and strength, and usually inspires a bit of slander from the peanut gallery. Once you're past the first-time beginner level of lead climbing and have a few days in the gym under your belt, spend time on easier climbs and focus not on the climbing but on clipping.

Watch expert climbers clip with lightning speed and try to emulate their style. At first, clipping fast may make the climbing feel slightly more strenuous, but with practice, you'll learn to relax while you clip quickly, and the fast clipping will make the climbing feel easier. To develop a fast clipping style, when you're on easier climbs, such as when you're warming up or getting in some mileage, feel free to climb slow, but clip as fast and efficiently as you possibly can.

You can also improve your clipping speed by learning to clip most of the time without putting the rope in your mouth. Not only is this really gross if you think about all the people biting gym ropes in the same spot and how much the ropes get dragged around the floor of the gym, but biting the rope also adds another step to the clip. Instead, reach down as far as you possibly can to grab the rope, let a bit slide

Avoid the dreaded Z-clip. Gym bolts are usually close enough together that it is easy to accidentally grab the rope from below the previous bolt and clip it in to the next bolt, creating a dramatic zigzag to the rope and quickly stopping upward fun.

through your hand if you need more rope, and slap it into the biner with conviction.

Let's say you are climbing a route that, from the ground, is obviously a knuckle-bending, tip-shredding crimp fest. In a few places, you have the choice of clipping from another crimper or an open-hand sloper. Which hold do you think will preserve your crimp power best? The sloper, of course.

Before you start up a route, and during a climb when you have a resting hold, take time to look ahead at where the climb goes relative to the bolts and other climbers.

This is easier said than done, as holding slopers often feels less secure than holding a crimper; but as long as the fall is safe, a smart climber will work out the foot and body position to clip from the slopers and save a few ounces of crimp power for the white-knuckle cruxes.

Additionally, gym routes are almost always sustained at the grade, so figuring out the most efficient positions to clip from can make the difference between a proud send and another whipper. When things get really pumpy, a common strategy is to *skip a clip*. While this can be a good strategy on sustained, long pitches outdoors, this method will get you a big fat FAIL on your lead test and is strongly discouraged and even expressly prohibited in some gyms. If you do skip a clip, do it *only* as a last resort and high on the wall where a longer fall is still safe!

CHOOSING WHEN TO CLIP

Better form than skipping a clip entirely is to clip at your waist as you pass the bolt. This saves almost as much power as skipping the clip entirely because you can integrate the clip into the motion of climbing and eliminate the time needed to pull up a bight of rope to clip. Clipping at the waist also requires careful assessment of fall length, nearby climbers, and fall trajectory because you will be a few feet higher above the previous bolt than you would be if you clipped while still below the bolt. In the most wickedly sustained terrain, clipping at the waist can actually be safer because a fall while clipping will not have the added length of an armload of slack. Falling with an armload of slack while trying to clip can cause shockingly long falls and should be avoided. The five feet of additional slack you pull up to clip can easily translate into fifteen feet of added fall length when all factors (rope stretch, belayer weight, and distance above previous bolt) are considered.

At the top of the wall, where forearms are burning and it feels like even the world's biggest hold is too small, it is tempting to reach up from below and clip the anchor. This isn't a safety concern, but it is a habit that will cost you many a strong performance. Nearly every gym route finishes by grabbing a friendly jug, or wrapping a hand over the top of the wall. No matter how tempted you are to stand on your tiptoes and lock-off at your belly button to clip the top anchor, don't. Instead, force yourself to go all the way to the finishing hold to clip the anchors. It's good for your mind and your performance.

The bottom line of climbing gym safety is to remember that gravity works just the same in the world's safest climbing gym as it does at the world's most dangerous outdoor climbing area. A mistake can be fatal, and just as with outdoor climbing, a smart climber will keep a part of their consciousness focused on safety at all times. Completely tied knots, attentive belaying, awareness of fall trajectory, and an overall sense of self-awareness are the keys to a long and healthy climbing career both indoors and out.

EXERCISE—CLIPPING ON LEAD

To learn to clip lead anchors more efficiently, choose a climb that is comfortably below your climbing limit and climb it two times in a row. The first time, clip each quickdraw with your left hand. The second time, clip each quickdraw with your right hand. If you find one hand is less proficient than the other, make a point of developing your weak-side clip by using your weak hand to clip during your warmup and at times when either hand can be used.

Opposite: *Kristen Felix on* Country Club Crack *(5.11), Colorado*

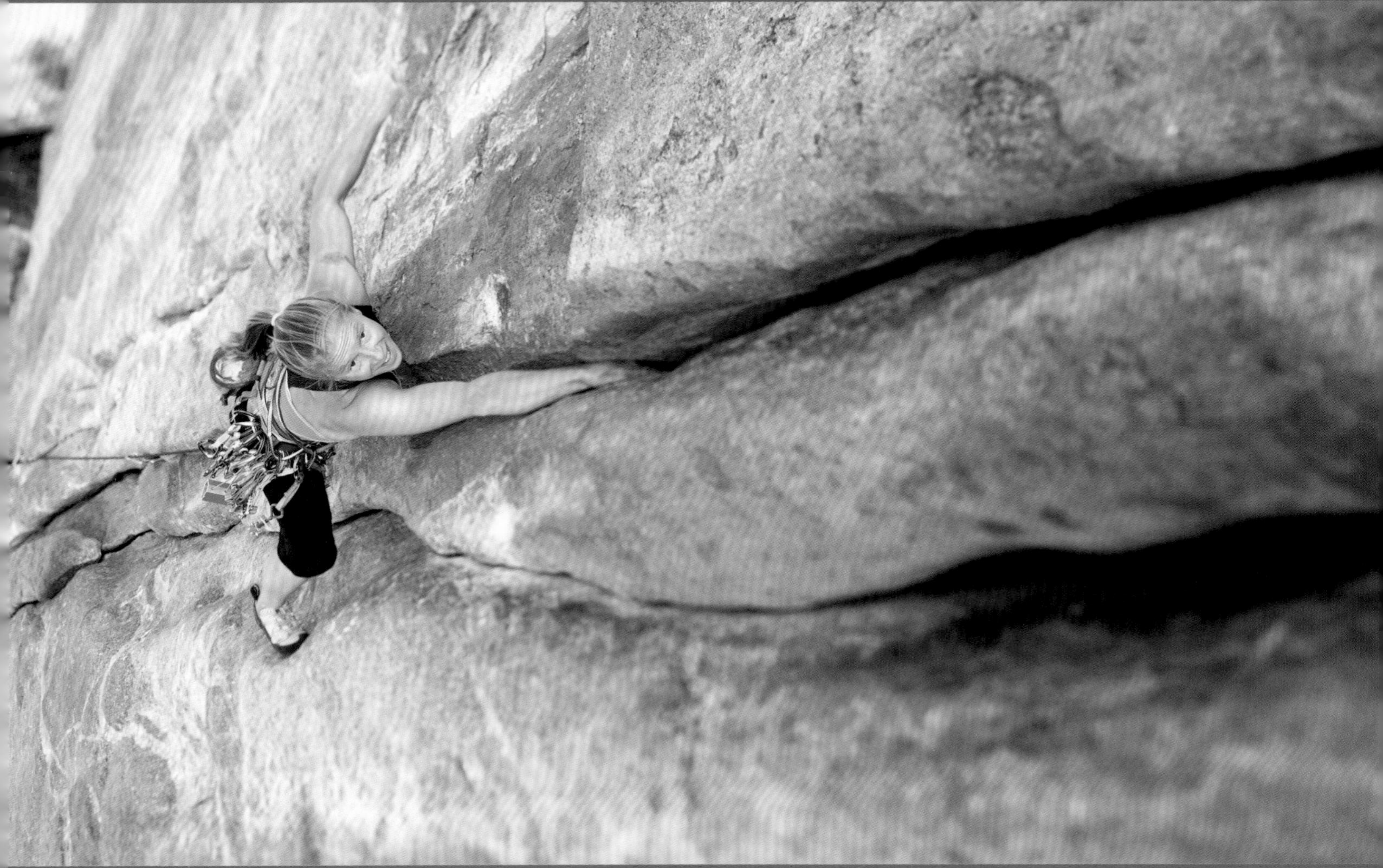

CHAPTER 9

Trad Leading

Trad climbing can provide a lot of fun and adventure in wild, airy places. Whether you're monkeying out roofs in the Gunks, racing up Half Dome in a day, taking a voyage into the murky depths of the Black Canyon, climbing dreamy granite spires in the Bugaboos, or even just enjoying a few pleasant pitches after work at any of the other hundreds of distinctive traditional climbing areas, one thing remains common: to lead trad routes safely you need good knowledge, judgment, and skills for protecting the climb. Every climb poses some risk to the leader; the goal is to manage that risk to an acceptable level while enjoying the climbing.

This chapter discusses the rack you should carry on a traditional route and how to strategically protect a climb, balancing safety with efficiency.

The chapter also covers
- setting the first piece in a pitch,
- protecting a pitch,
- using quickdraws and slings to minimize rope drag,
- using half ropes to reduce rope drag,
- the duties of a leader.

Red River Gorge, Kentucky, is famous for its relentlessly overhanging sandstone sport routes, but it also has some superb trad cragging. Say you're at "the Red," gearing up to climb the classic crack *B3* (5.11b). From the ground, you can see that it's going to be mostly a finger and hand crack, but the crack appears to get smaller up high. Because it's only a one-pitch route, you cut the rack down to shave weight. A selection of wired nuts, micronuts, a couple of hexes, some tiny cams, and a double set of finger- to hand-size cams will be more than sufficient.

The climbing goes smoothly, jamming the perfect crack in stellar rock. You set most of the pro from decent stances to save mental and physical energy for the crux. The climbing is pretty straight up, so you clip the cams and hexes directly, and you clip the nuts with a quickdraw. You set the nuts and hexes whenever the crack allows, keeping the precious cams for when the placements get strenuous.

The crack becomes less pro-friendly at the crux. By looking ahead, you anticipate

Traditional racks:

A big rack can be distributed between the gear sling and the harness.

For steeper rock, racking on the harness is usually better because the gear you need doesn't swing so far out of reach behind you.

On moderate multipitch climbs and off-widths, a shoulder sling is usually best because it is easy to push out of the way and is fast for passing the rack to the other climber when swapping leads.

the difficulty, so you set two good pieces where the crack is still good, and you take a rest. Then you go for it—the pitch is sheer, with nothing to hit if you fall. You could try to wriggle in little nuts to reduce the runout, but that would take a lot of energy and actually increase the chance of falling, and the pro wouldn't be good anyway. Better just to climb through. With the last cam well below your feet, you toss the rare trad dyno to slap the horizontal break. Once on this ledge, you get some reprieve before launching into the intricate final moves. You set one piece immediately to end the runout below and another as high as you

can to keep yourself off the ledge in a fall, squeak through the awkward stemming moves, and clip the fixed tree anchor.

Strategy is key for leading a trad route like *B3* safely. It's important to protect the route efficiently so that you have enough strength for both climbing and placing the protection. It's far easier to climb dangerously, and you might even get away with it for a while, but in the long run, it's far better to put in the effort and discipline to climb every pitch as safely and efficiently as you can. Practicing this kind of strategy every time you climb makes it easier to make good decisions when the climbing is difficult and

the protection, tricky. This is particularly true for climbers just breaking in to more difficult terrain. Far too often, aspiring 5.10 or 5.11 trad leaders end up taking dangerous or even injurious falls after finding themselves too pumped to manage the protection and trying to climb their way to safety without placing enough gear.

TRAD CLIMBING GEAR SELECTION

On traditional climbs, the leader needs quite a selection of gear for setting protection and building belay anchors. What you bring depends on the style and preferences of the climbing team and the requirements of the route. The rack described below is a good starting point for many multipitch traditional routes. It covers a range of crack sizes and provides plenty of slings, quickdraws, and carabiners for extending protection and setting belays. A typical trad climbing rack may include the following:

- one or two sets of wired nuts
- two or three hexes
- one or two sets of cams ranging from 1–7.6 centimeters (⅜–3 inches)
- seven to ten quickdraws
- five to eight shoulder-length slings
- one or two double-length slings
- six to eight extra carabiners
- two to four locking carabiners
- one or two cordelettes
- one gear sling (some climbers prefer to rack on the harness)
- one nut tool

This basic rack can get you safely up many routes, and when a guidebook suggests a "standard rack" this is usually what it means. You might beef up the rack if the route has long pitches and include some bigger gear if the climb has wide cracks. If you anticipate short pitches or abundant fixed anchors, pare the rack down to save weight—it's much easier to climb with a light rack.

Seek information about recommended gear from a guidebook, internet forums, other climbers, and by scoping the route from the ground. Take all this information with a grain of salt—guidebooks can be wrong, internet beta is notoriously inaccurate, other climbers can give well-intentioned but faulty information, and even the view from the ground can be misleading. Bring a little extra gear if you have doubts about your information; remember that cracks often look smaller than their true size when viewed from the ground and constantly assess your retreat options in case things don't work as planned.

PROTECTING THE CLIMB

Protecting a climb is part science, part art. You have a lot of creativity open to you, but you have to get a few basic things right. Having gear that's in good condition and well organized by size on the rack will make the job easier.

The leader manages a fine line, using judgment to assess and mitigate risk while climbing with confidence and efficiency.

Opposite: *Marc Gay is all smiles on* Sinners on Sunday *(5.12), Mt. Evans, Colorado.*

Some climbers overdo the analysis and protection, and it holds them back. Too many complicated systems or too much hesitation and doubt will climb a team right into the afternoon thunderstorm. To climb harder trad routes, you need to be quick and confident with your protection.

FIRST PROTECTION

Once you get a few feet above the ground (or if the landing is rough and the climbing hard, maybe even while standing on the ground), it's time to start setting protection. The first protection in a pitch can receive a strong outward pull, depending on the position of the belayer. If this first piece pops out, the outward pull goes to the next piece higher—and it's possible to zipper out several pieces this way. To avoid this, the first piece should be able to hold a downward pull to protect the climber, *and* an outward pull to protect the pieces above. A good cam, two pieces opposed, or another multidirectional placement that can withstand an outward pull is a smart first piece.

On a multipitch route, the leader should set good protection as soon as possible above the belay. The first piece (or two) of protection is one of the most crucial pieces—it protects the belay anchors from a hard impact and it makes the catch easier for the belayer. If the climbing is hard, many experienced climbers will put a couple of pieces right next to each other just above the belay to ensure

If the first piece fails the outward pull, the other pieces may, too, and they could "zipper" on up the rope.

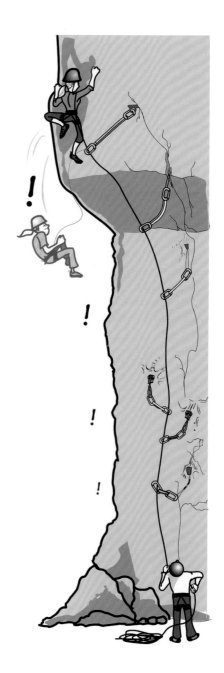

You can clip the top piece in the belay. The individual placements must be bomber for this to be safe—but you want bomber pieces in your belay anchors anyway!

While it's wise to clip protection early in the pitch to avoid a factor-2 fall onto the anchors, the jury is still out on whether it's smart to clip your belay anchors as the first piece of protection. While it should make the catch easier for the belayer, it also increases forces on the anchors by 60–70 percent because of the pulley effect. If the anchors aren't stellar, you might not want to clip in to them for lead protection. If the placements are truly bomber, it is probably a good idea to clip the top one as lead protection.

that a hard fall onto the belay anchor will not happen. As noted in chapter 1, recent studies show that a factor-2 fall is likely to injure the belayer or hit them with so much force that they lose control of the rope.

Depending on the arrangement of the anchor and your belayer, you can clip either the top shelf for the first protection or a higher placement in the belay. Sometimes, especially when it's easy climbing above a good belay ledge, it's better to climb up a little way to set the first protection. When the climbing is hard or runout off

Ahhh . . . that's better. Things get safer for the team once the leader sets solid protection above the belay. This reduces the fall factor, the impact force, and the pull on the belayer; and it protects the belay anchors from a high impact. The leader has to keep setting protection at reasonable intervals to continue reducing the fall factor and the potential force.

the belay, it can be safer to place the first piece above the belay while leading and still on belay from the previous pitch. Clip the piece and then climb back down to the belay. This is particularly useful on bolted climbs, where the second can be belayed through the first bolt of the next pitch and then get a handy top rope for the first few moves of the next lead. Like many things

in climbing, it's entirely up to you and your partner to make the call.

PROTECTING THE PITCH

The leader sets protection as the pitch unfolds. At the beginning of the pitch, set gear frequently to protect against a ground fall. On easy terrain, it can be tempting to run it out off the belay, but no matter the grade, do everything possible to place good protection frequently near the belay and save your boldness for another time. As you get higher up the pitch, you can space the protection more and get your runout on, provided that there are no ledges to hit. Whenever you pass a ledge, place protection close together again for a few pieces to keep you off the ledge if you fall.

When you get to a point with a crux looming just above, place a couple of good pieces if possible. When the climbing is hard, more protection keeps you safer and helps keep your head relaxed. It's smart to always have at least two bomber pieces between you and a bad fall. If the protection isn't great, place more. Aside from safety, placing a couple of bomber pieces at the beginning of a hard section can make the difference between really going for it and slumping onto a piece of protection because you "didn't trust you gear."

If the rock is solid and the climbing is easy, you can get by with less protection, but you don't want to run it out too far. After falling 45 feet, a 150-pound climber will be doing nearly 40 miles per hour and carrying about 10 kN (or over 2,000 pounds) of potential force. The rope stretch and belayer give will reduce the final impact force, but making huge runouts is not heroic; it makes the entire team vulnerable to a broken hold or slip. Your partner counts on you to make good decisions and lead the pitch safely, not get hasty, fall, and create an epic. Climbers who regularly push the limits of their ability and protection are rolling the dice. This may seem alarmist, but leader falls are all-too-common causes of accidents in rock climbing according to *Accidents in North American Mountaineering.*

Set plenty of protection on traverses, especially before and after the cruxes—gear before the crux protects the leader, gear after the crux protects the second. If you've just climbed up a ways and are beginning a traverse, set a directional anchor to keep the rope above the second climber through the vertical section. You can also set protection to show your partner where to go or to keep the rope away from bad rock, sharp edges, or rope-eating cracks. The potential forces of a pendulum fall are almost the same as a free fall. In a laboratory, a 150-pound weight dropped from a point level with but 30 feet to the side of the anchor point will be going close to 30 miles per hour at the bottom of the pendulum. The actual physics of a climbing fall's speed will vary, depending on rope stretch, climber friction against the rock, angle of the rock, and rope out between climber and belayer, but the point is that hitting a flake or rock wall at the bottom of a 30-foot pendulum is not so different from hitting the ground from 30 feet up and would likely result in injury. If the climber is at a 45-degree angle

Steph Davis cruising Quarter of a Man *(5.12), Indian Creek, Utah. Protecting this pitch involves using a good strategy for being both safe and efficient.*

Finger cracks often deliver some of the most solid gear and most enjoyable gymnastics in the world of climbing.

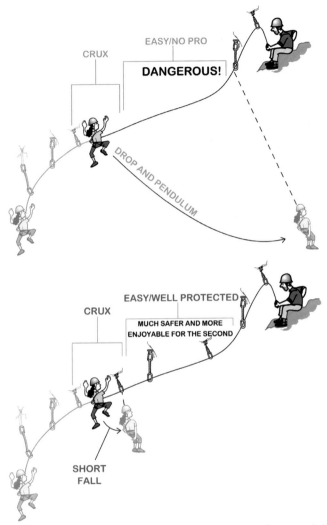

CRUX

EASY/NO PRO

DANGEROUS!

DROP AND PENDULUM

EASY/WELL PROTECTED

CRUX

MUCH SAFER AND MORE
ENJOYABLE FOR THE SECOND

SHORT
FALL

Set plenty of protection on traverses, especially after the cruxes, or else the second climber can take a big pendulum fall.

to their protection, or pendulum point, the speed of fall will be about half that of the fall described above, but still enough to cause injury. As the distance from the protection point increases at any given angle, so does the potential speed of fall. At times it will be safest for the second climber to climb past the protection, which can protect them from the swing, then reach back and clean it from better holds.

When you find yourself following a pitch like this, you'll appreciate a leader who placed protection not only for himself but also for you.

A clever leader will use protection to keep a rope from running into a tight crack, especially at the lip of a roof. Pro can be set to pull the rope away from the crack, as shown here, or it can be set inside the crack to keep the rope out. A nut, chock, or Big Bro—whichever fits the crack—works well for this.

ADVANCED TIP—EXTENDABLE QUICKDRAWS

Extendable quickdraws are handy on alpine and traditional rock routes. When the route runs straight up, you can leave the quickdraw shortened to minimize the length of a fall. When more extension is needed to keep the rope running clean, simply extend the sling.

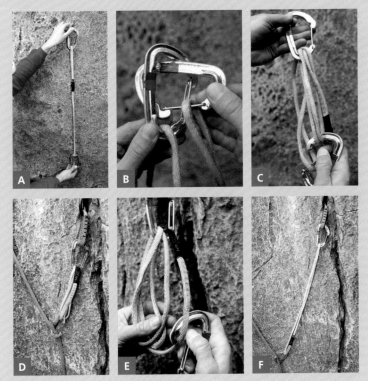

A. Clip two carabiners in to a shoulder-length sling and pull them apart onto opposite sides of the sling.

B. Pass one of the carabiners through the interior of the other.

C. Pull the carabiner down until it is even with the two new loops in the sling and clip them.

D. Now you have an extendable quickdraw.

E. You can quickly get full extension by unclipping any two strands . . .

F. . . . and pulling the sling apart.

DUTIES OF THE LEADER

- Research the route's ascent and descent information, gear requirements, and current conditions.
- Come prepared with the right gear and a good mental state.
- Double-check knots, buckles, and belay setups before taking off on lead.
- Set good protection right above the belay.
- Climb efficiently and in control.
- Set solid protection early and often in the pitch.
- Stay aware of the ever-changing consequences of a fall, depending on ledges and the ground, and protect accordingly.
- Exploit obvious protection opportunities, and ferret out obscure ones when necessary.
- Stay on route.
- Protect traverses for the second as well as the leader and communicate with the second on how to clean the traverse safely.
- Use appropriate extension to keep the rope running straight, but don't overextend the protection.
- Avoid placing protection where it creates rope drag.
- Try to keep the rope away from bad rock, sharp edges, and rope-eating cracks.
- If the protection is sketchy or nonexistent, climb in absolute control or find a safe way to bail off the route.
- Find a good belay station at the end of each pitch.
- Watch the weather and execute contingency plans if the weather goes sour or if the climbing is too hard or dangerous.

Extension

On a straight-up pitch, it's usually okay to clip the rope directly in to the slings of cams or to clip wired nuts with a quick-draw. If the pitch traverses or climbs over a roof or jogs right or left, however, it's good to extend the protection to keep the rope running straight. Try to get just the right length of extension—too much extension will increase the length of a fall more than necessary.

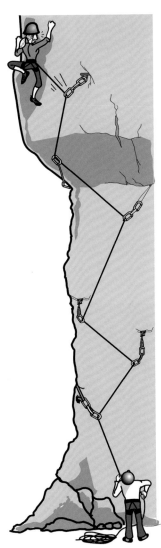

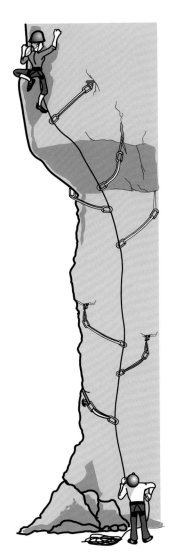

Poor extension. The protection is not extended enough, so the rope makes many bends back and forth. This creates huge rope drag and also puts a sideways pulling force on the pieces, which could pull them out in a fall.

Good extension. The rope runs clean by adding appropriate extension to the protection pieces.

On straight-up cracks, it's best to clip a cam directly if it's not buried deep in the crack. This also minimizes the length of a potential fall. Here, the leader ensures minimal rope drag with a combination of clipping short while the crack was going straight up, then with long slings just before the climb traversed right.

On this sharp turn right, it's good to sling the protection extra long to prevent the rope from bending too sharply. Two shoulder slings enchained are necessary to avoid rope drag here.

BAD

Here, even this slight bend in the rope will cause horrific rope drag for the leader as they climb above.

In this case, just a single quickdraw extension is enough to keep the rope running straight.

ADVANCED TIP—HALF ROPES

On wandering routes, half ropes work great for clipping selective pieces—one rope on the right and the other on the left—to keep the ropes running clean. If two ropes are needed to descend anyway, the half-rope system can be the way to go. If the team must haul gear, though, a single rope and haul line work better.

By clipping one rope to the left and one to the right, it's possible to keep the ropes running straight without extending the protection much. Half-rope technique also gives you a backup if one rope severs, but it can be more cumbersome dealing with two ropes, and cases of rope cutting are exceedingly rare. Most climbing is done using single-rope technique.

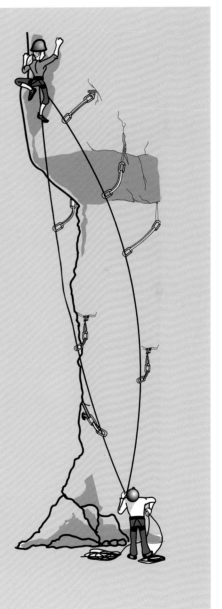

EXERCISE—TRAD PROTECTION

Beginning Trad Leader: The safest way to start trad leading is to do a few mock leads, with a top rope and a guide or *very* experienced trad climber to clean and evaluate your protection. The assignment: perform four mock leads to see if you're ready to move on to the real deal. The first couple of leads should be easy, so you can relax while you set the gear. The next two leads should be progressively harder to give you a feel of what it's like to place gear under pressure. If the climber or guide who evaluates your gear gives the green light, it's time to do some real leads. For your first climbs, choose routes with ample protection opportunities that are easy for you to climb and slowly progress to harder climbs.

Intermediate Trad Leader: Improve your protection-setting skills: go to the base of an area that has plenty of cracks and set as much protection as you can in ten or fifteen minutes and have your partner evaluate the placements. Set all the types of gear that you have on your rack; don't fall into the "cams only" mind-set. Repeat the exercise in different spots until you can quickly set a variety of good protection. Then, when climbing, challenge yourself to pick the right piece the first time rather than always taking several attempts to match the cam or chock with the crack size.

Advanced Trad Leader: On a short pitch that is entirely visible from the ground, try selecting the exact rack you will need before you leave the ground. Carry some extra gear on the back of your harness in case you get it wrong. This will help you to anticipate gear needs, which improves protection strategy, confidence in making do with what you have, and reduces the need to carry tons of extra equipment on longer pitches.

Opposite: *Tommy Caldwell going for a 40-footer on* Broken Brain *(5.12), Indian Creek, Utah*

CHAPTER 10

Climbing Forces

Climbing is bound by the laws of physics. Physics determines how a climbing move should be made, whether or not your foot will stick on a hold, and why a cam holds a fall. Physics also determines how much force is generated in a climbing fall. The thing about climbing physics is that although it deals with relatively simple concepts (like gravity), the real-world physics of climbing gear and climbing gymnastics is extremely complex.

This chapter discusses

- Newton's laws of motion and how they relate to a falling climber,
- how gravitational potential energy becomes kinetic energy—the energy of motion—in a fall,
- how the belay method can drastically affect the impact force in a leader fall,
- what the fall factor is and how it influences impact force,
- how the UIAA tests ropes to measure their impact force.

For some climbers, enduring this chapter might be more painful than grinding up a feldspar-lined off-width. If you find your eyes rolling up into your head, your eyelids drooping, or your brain screaming for diversion, don't worry. Just start with the sidebar on relevant lessons, drop the book, load your pack, and go climbing—but while you're at it, study the physics of gear placements, direction of pull, fall trajectories, and climber/belayer weight differences. If you're a true glutton, a student of physics, or just really bored, read on for a deeper understanding of climbing physics.

NEWTON'S LAWS OF MOTION

Issac Newton pondered a falling apple. He may as well have considered a falling climber while devising his laws of motion, which define the motion of bodies.

The rate of acceleration of an object is proportional to the force applied to the object. Gravity definitely seems to tug harder some days than others, but it actually pulls us toward the earth's center with a constant force that is equal to our body weight. In a free fall, gravity accelerates a falling climber's body at 9.8 meters

THE RELEVANT LESSONS OF THIS CHAPTER

The highest impact forces on the protection, climber, and belayer occur when the leader falls close to the belay, with only a little rope out from the belayer to stretch and absorb energy.

Setting good protection early in the pitch, and regularly thereafter, significantly decreases the forces on the anchors, the climber, and the belayer in a fall. The early protection also prevents a factor-2 fall onto the belay anchors.

A dynamic belay, where some rope slips through the belay device when a fall is being stopped, can drastically reduce the force in a high-impact fall.

per second^2 (32.2 feet per second^2). Thus, a climber in free fall will fall 4.9 meters the first second, and because the falling climber is accelerating and not continuing at the same speed, they will fall three times farther the next second, and five times farther the third second. The body accelerates for about five seconds until it reaches approximately 122 miles (196 kilometers) per hour—terminal velocity: the speed where wind drag balances gravitational pull.

A falling climber accelerates at 9.8 meters per second^2 until the rope arrests the fall. If the rope were a cable, the climber would halt almost instantly; the rapid deceleration would create a massive impact force on the climber and the protection, damaging the climber's internal organs and blowing out the climbing anchors. Dynamic climbing ropes stretch to control the climber's rate of deceleration, thereby limiting the impact force on the climber and the gear.

Every action has an equal and opposite reaction. When we stand, the ground pushes up with a force equal and opposite to our body weight. While climbing, the hand- and footholds support a force equal to our weight (when we use the holds to oppose each other, they support more than body weight). In a fall, the rope creates a force to catch us; this is called the impact force. The impact force on the rope pulls on the belayer, who must oppose the rope's pull. The top anchor holds a force equal to that of the climber and the belayer combined (if we ignore rope drag), and the rock surrounding the top anchor opposes the forces created by the anchor—hopefully—or else the anchor fails. The forces created in a lead fall begin with the falling climber, then transfer through the rope to the belayer, anchors, and ultimately the rock to fulfill the equal-and-opposite reaction of Newton's third law.

POTENTIAL AND KINETIC ENERGY

When climbing, you work to move your body mass upward against gravity. Some of the energy used to climb becomes gravitational *potential energy*—energy stored due to the pull of gravity and your position above

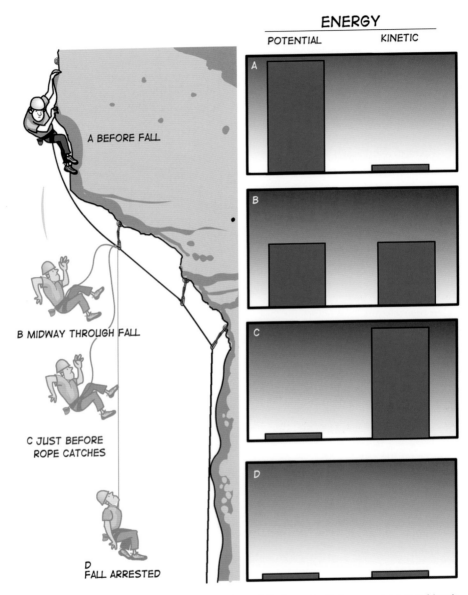

As you climb, you store more potential energy. If you fall, the potential energy becomes kinetic energy, the energy of motion.

the earth. If you take a leader fall, potential energy quickly converts to *kinetic energy*—the energy of motion—as gravity accelerates your body downward. The farther you fall, the faster you go, as your body's potential energy becomes kinetic energy.

Herein lies the double whammy of "running it out": a longer fall increases the chance of hitting something and increases the speed at which you hit it. The more speed you have, the more energy available to smash your bones if you hit a ledge.

Setting protection decreases the length and speed of a potential fall. The obvious conclusion: more protection means more safety . . . to a point. More protection also means more time spent fiddling with gear, more physical and mental energy devoured, and more gear carried. Every leader should seek a balance between safety and efficiency.

In a clean fall on a vertical or overhanging face with no ledges to hit, the rope absorbs most of the energy by stretching. Some energy also goes into overcoming rope friction from the carabiners and the rock, and perhaps lifting the belayer. If the impact force is high, some energy might go into forcing the rope to slip through the belay device and belayer's hand, provided that she's belaying with a device that does not lock the rope. If the fall isn't clean and the climber hits a ledge, much of the energy can go into breaking his bones.

When top-roping, a fall is halted almost immediately. A short fall creates less chance of hitting something, and it also limits the amount of potential energy

transformed into kinetic energy, so the speed of the fall is slow. This is what makes top-roping so safe.

IMPACT FORCE

In a lead fall, the climber's body exerts an impact force on the rope that must be countered by the belayer. Friction at the high carabiner and from the rope running over the rock and through other protection allows the belayer to feel less impact force than the leader. The force on the top protection equals the force on the climber and the belayer combined. The magnitude of the impact force created is largely determined by

- the belay method,
- the fall factor,
- body weight,
- rope elongation.

BELAY METHOD

A dynamic belay, where some rope slips through the tube- or plate-belay device as the fall is stopped, arrests a fall more gradually. This can dramatically decrease the impact force in a fall with a high fall factor (see next section). The dynamic belay is usually unintentional—a belayer's hand can hold only so much force, so some rope automatically slips in a hard fall. A good belayer might also intentionally let some rope slip through the device if the climb is overhanging so that the climber does not smack the wall as hard.

If the belayer uses an assisted-braking device, the rope locks tight in a fall. If the belayer is also tightly anchored, the belay

Using an assisted-braking belay device in conjunction with an upward-pull anchor as shown here creates a very static belay, particularly when there is not much rope between the belayer and the leader. This could cause marginal pieces to fail or cause the leader to swing violently into the wall.

will be almost totally static and will create the highest impact force possible for that fall. Assisted-braking belay devices should be used only when the protection is bomber, such as on well-bolted sport climbs or trad routes with perfect crack protection. Even

on such routes, climbers should be aware that the impact force can be massive if the leader falls while close to the belay. On overhanging climbs, a static belay can cause the leader to swing hard into the wall, a mistake that has caused numerous broken ankles.

If the belayer is on flat ground and using an assisted-braking device, she can jump up as the force of the fall comes onto her. This is similar to having some rope slip through the belay device; it adds some dynamics to the belay and decreases the impact force. These differences are significant. A larger belayer will need to intentionally move upward with the force of a fall in order to prevent a hard fall by a smaller climber. Larger belayers can provide soft catches with an assisted-braking device by standing a short distance away from the wall and stepping or jumping upward as the force of the fall hits the end of the rope. An easier and more reliable way for a larger belayer to give a softer (more dynamic) catch is to use a regular tube or plate device.

FALL FACTOR

The higher the fall factor, the greater the impact force in a fall. The important concept of the fall factor is that falls close to the belay create the highest forces because only a little rope exists between the belayer and the climber to absorb the energy of the fall. As the leader gets higher up the pitch, more rope comes into the system to stretch and absorb energy, so the force created in a fall decreases (provided that the leader has regularly placed protection).

$$\text{Fall Factor} = \frac{\text{vertical distance fallen}}{\text{length of rope out}}$$

The fall factor takes into account the amount of energy released in a fall and the length of rope available to absorb it. Two falls with equal fall factors theoretically create the same impact force regardless of the distance fallen (if the rope, climber weight, and belay method remain the same). Obviously, a longer fall might be more dangerous because of the increased chance of hitting something, but the forces generated are similar because the long fall has more rope available to absorb energy. The longer fall is also more severe because the force impacts the climber and anchors for a longer time.

A true factor-2 fall can occur only when the leader is directly above the belay on a vertical wall with no protection, so the fall is twice the length of the rope out. A factor-2 fall creates the greatest force possible on the climber and belayer if the belayer is using a device that allows minimal rope slippage. If the belayer is using a tube or plate device, rope will slip through the device, which significantly decreases the forces but could burn the brake hand of the belayer. The force of such a fall comes directly onto the belayer and the belay anchors, making it a hard catch and creating an exceptionally high load on the belay anchors. Recent studies have shown that true factor-2 falls cause enough force to injure the belayer—it is best to climb in such a way that you never take a factor-2 fall. Safe climbers avoid factor-2 falls by setting solid protection just above the belay and by climbing with a free soloist's control if a runout off the belay is necessary. The first few pieces of protection in a pitch are critical because they decrease the fall factor and back up the belay anchors.

As you climb up a pitch, more rope feeds into the system. More rope means more capacity to absorb energy. A 10-foot fall from 100 feet above the belay creates substantially less force than a 10-foot fall near the belay, because the rope stretches more in the longer fall.

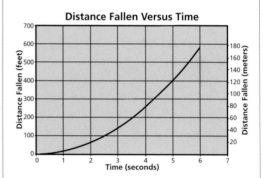

Distance Fallen Versus Time

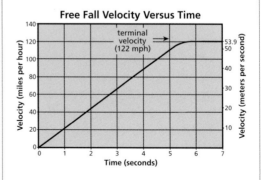

Free Fall Velocity Versus Time

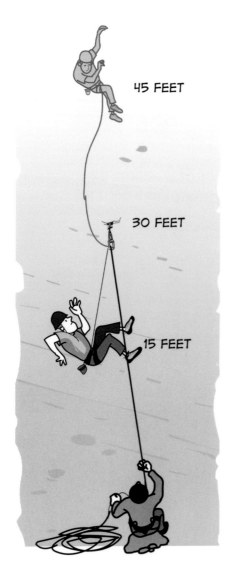

45 FEET

30 FEET

15 FEET

The fall factor is the distance that you fall divided by the amount of rope out. In this case, a 30-foot fall on 45 feet of rope makes a fall factor of 0.67.

BODY WEIGHT

On any given day, your body weight is a fixed amount; gear and clothing add to your effective weight. Larger climbers create higher impact forces when they fall, so they might consider climbing on thicker ropes and placing extra protection or setting beefier belay anchors in some situations.

ROPE ELONGATION

A dynamic lead rope is really just a long spring. When a rope catches a fall, most of the kinetic energy goes into stretching the rope and is ultimately dissipated as heat that is caused by friction between the rope fibers; some of the energy even transforms into molecular changes in the rope fibers.

As you climb higher up a pitch, the length of rope between the climber and the belayer increases. More rope out means more capacity for the rope to stretch and absorb energy, which results in a lower impact force and a longer fall. Some ropes stretch more than others to give a soft catch; these low-impact-force ropes decrease the force on the protection, climber, and belayer, but the extra stretch might increase your chances of hitting a ledge.

As a dynamic climbing rope catches a fall, the force on the climber, belayer, and anchors builds as the rope stretches. At the instant when the rope reaches its maximum stretch, the load reaches its maximum impact force. Then the force diminishes until the top anchor holds only the climber's weight and some of the belayer's weight.

MOMENTUM AND IMPULSE

The *momentum* of an object equals its mass times its velocity. The faster an object is moving or the heavier it is, the more momentum it has. If you graph the impact force as it grows from zero to the peak force, the area under the curve equals the *impulse,* which is the change of a falling climber's momentum. You can calculate the impulse by multiplying the climber's mass by his change in velocity.

A falling climber slows from maximum velocity the instant the rope begins arresting the fall to zero velocity once the fall stops, which occurs at the instant of peak force. The change in velocity, therefore, equals the maximum velocity reached in the fall, because the final velocity is zero. In a clean fall, the length of the fall determines the maximum velocity.

Halting a fall creates a given impulse—equal to the climber's mass times the maximum falling velocity. As mentioned above, this is the area under the force-versus-time curve. A static rope stretches little, so it stops a leader fall quickly. The rapid arrest drives

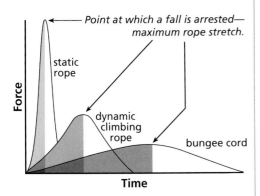

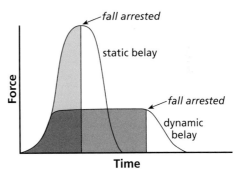

The static rope doesn't stretch much in a leader fall, so the duration of the impulse is short, causing the impact force to spike. A dynamic climbing rope stretches enough to keep the forces reasonable without dropping the climber too far. A bungee cord, on the other hand, stretches so much that the time to arrest the fall is relatively long. This keeps the impact force low but increases the length of the fall so much that the climber is likely to get battered on the way down.

A dynamic belay increases the time to arrest the fall, thereby decreasing the impact force. A static belay halts the fall rapidly, creating a much higher peak force. The impulse is the same for either belay method, so the area under the force-versus-time curves is equal.

UIAA ROPE TESTS

The UIAA (Union of International Alpine Associations) conducts severe drop tests on ropes. These tests are much harsher than most real-life falls, so they provide a conservative measure of a rope's suitability for climbing. During the tests, they drop an 80-kilogram (175-pound) mass 1.8 meters (6 feet) onto a 2.8-meter-long (9-foot-long) piece of rope (the test mass is dropped 1 meter from above the anchor point). They drop the test mass repeatedly every five minutes until the rope breaks.

A single rope must hold at least five falls, and the first drop must not exceed 12 kN (2,700 pounds) of impact force on the "climber." If the rope does not stretch enough, the impact force will be too high for the rope to pass the test. In a real fall, if the rope didn't stretch enough, the impact force could damage the climber's internal organs and break the climbing protection. Each subsequent drop causes a higher impact force because the rope loses some of its elasticity. This is why it's smart to switch ends or let your rope "rest" a few minutes after taking a high-impact fall.

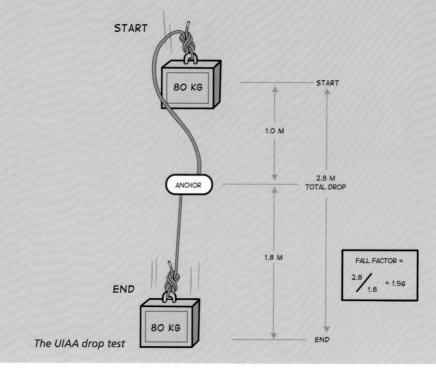

The UIAA drop test

Lilla Molnar pondering fall potential during a first ascent in the Purcell Mountains, Canada

the force to stratospheric levels because less time slowing and stopping the fall means more force is required. In contrast, in a fall on a bungee cord, the huge elongation spreads the deceleration over a much longer time. The slow deceleration keeps the impact force low, but the impulse—the area under the force-versus-time curve—is the same as with the static rope. Bungee cords wouldn't work well for climbing, though, because falls would be too long.

A dynamic climbing rope is a compromise between the static cord and the bungee. It stretches just enough to keep impact forces in worst-case falls within a range that the human body can tolerate. A dynamic rope creates the same impulse to stop a falling climber as a static rope or a bungee, but it creates much less force than a static rope and stretches far less than a bungee.

STRENGTH OF CLIMBING GEAR

Climbing gear is designed to be functional, light, and able to withstand climbing falls.

The list below shows the range of strengths for various pieces of gear from different manufacturers.

CLIMBING GEAR STRENGTH RANGE		
	kilonewtons	pounds
Nuts and Cams		
Micronuts	2–7	450–1,575
Small wired nuts	4–7	900–1,575
Medium wired nuts	6–12	1,350–2,700
Large wired nuts	10–12	2,250–2,700
Small cams	3–10	675–2,250
Cams	12–14	2,700–3,150
Rope	18–22	4,000–5,000
Carabiners		
Full strength	23–25	5,175–5,625
Gate-open strength	7–10	1,575–2,250
Cross-loaded strength	7–10	1,575–2,250
Locking carabiners	23–30	5,175–6,750
High-Strength Cord		
5.5–6 millimeter	14–21	3,150–4,800
Nylon Cord		
5 millimeter	5–5.7	1,134–1,280
6 millimeter	7.4–8.7	1,653–1,955
7 millimeter	10–14	2,250–3,210
Webbing Slings		
8–12 millimeter Spectra/Dyneema	22	4,950
18 millimeter nylon	22	4,950

EXERCISE—FALL CALCULATOR

Several fall-force calculators can be found online. Search for "climbing fall-force cal-culator." With the fall calculator, you can plug in certain variables, such as the belay technique, the type of protection, the weight of the leader, the diameter of the rope, and the distance the leader is above the protection and the belay, and you'll get back theoretical impact forces on the climber, belayer, and top anchor.

Although the calculations for impact force are extremely simplified compared to reality (and in some cases you may get significant errors), it's still enlightening to change the variables around and see how this affects the impact force.

Acknowledgments

First and foremost, I'd like to thank Craig Luebben, who wrote the first edition of this book and did as much as anyone in history to shape the way climbing is taught—and the way climbing is learned. Craig's efforts to clarify the best practices in easy-to-understand ways made climbing a safer sport, accessible to more people. Craig was a visionary and positive force for the mainstream acceptance, and even adulation, of the sport we see today. Second, I'd like to thank Silvia Luebben, who trusted me to write the second edition of this book.

I also owe a big thank-you, and a belay, to all the climbers who appear in the photos in this book, including: Berndt Arnold, Mike Auldridge, Cassie Beermann, Francisco Blanco, Cassie Bloss, Katie Brown, Krystal Burnham, Robbie Burnham, Tommy Caldwell, Stacy Carrera, Joe Crocker, Cameron Cross, Micah Dash, Steph Davis, Aya Donahue, Anthony Everhardt, Rich Farnham, Kristin Felix, Marc Gay, Patience Gribble, Brittany Griffith, Sarah Gross, Skip Harper, Kennan Harvey, Lynn Hill, Alex Honnold, Brad Jackson, Andy Johnson, Sue Kligerman, David Lazaroff, Bill Libertore, Curtis Love, Giulia Luebben, Silvia Luebben, Charlie Mace, Anna McConica, Carol McConica, Jeremy Medley, Jared Ogden, Timmy O'Neill, Annette Oshana, Pascal Perrier, Kathy Plate, Beth Rodden, Eric Roed, Mike Schlauch, Vera Schulte-Pelkum, Jason Schultz, Jeff Skoloda, Laura Strauss, Kevin Stricker, Lauri Stricker, Anna Thomas, Toti Valdez, Matt Wade, Heidi Wirtz, and Gerald Zauner.

I am indebted to the editorial team at Mountaineers Books for their ongoing commitment to the highest standards of outdoor publishing, and, more specifically, for the oversight of Kate Rogers, who gave me enough freedom for inspiration and enough oversight for excellence; the project management of Emily White; the efficient and thorough editing of Erin Cusick; and the design expertise of McKenzie Long. And thanks to Metolius Climbing, DMM, Edelrid, Black Diamond, Fixe, Totem, Camp, and LaSportiva for providing equipment for the photos in this book; and EVO Louisville and the Boulder Rock Club for offering their indoor climbing facilities to be photographed.

This second edition preserves much of Craig's original voice and vision and some of the photos from the first edition. His appreciation for those who helped with the first edition includes Malcom Daly, for giving Craig his first guiding job; Gary Neptune, for the photos of historical equipment; the American Mountain Guides Association; Jim Ewing of Sterling Rope Company, for tests that showed cordelettes don't equalize as well as was first thought; John Long, for introducing Craig to climbing instructional books; Chuck Grossman, for the inspiration behind the Big Bro expandable tube chock that Craig invented as part of his mechanical engineering thesis at Colorado State University; and his wife, Silvia, and daughter, Giulia.

I also owe a debt of gratitude to the climbers and guides who, way back when I was a teenager, were willing to let a kid tag along on their climbing adventures around Estes Park in the days before it was cool to be a kid who climbed. These include Diane Russell, Keith Lober, Harry Kent, Larry Day, Scott Kimball, Rusty George, Michael Covington, Doug Snively, Bill McKee, Mike Caldwell, and Randy Farris. You all taught me more than you can imagine—about climbing and otherwise.

Finally, thanks to my father, Mike Donahue, whose favorite thing in the world was to show people a great adventure in the mountains. He loved climbing, but even more than climbing, he loved guiding. While growing up, I spent countless days accompanying him as he led people from all walks of life on mountain adventures. On these adventures with my dad, I climbed with strong climbers, weak climbers, bold climbers, timid climbers, disabled climbers, climbers who climbed only once and climbers who made it a lifelong pursuit, climbers who were terrified of heights, and climbers who never would have dreamed of standing on a rocky summit were it not for the soft, encouraging voice of my dad.

On those days with my dad, I learned many things about staying safe in the vertical world and about what motivates people to climb, and perhaps the most valuable lesson of all was that *anyone can climb*. And for that, I owe the sport itself an enormous thank-you. I know of no other outdoor sport where a person can try it for the very first time and have exactly the same experience as an expert. The cutting edge makes for good photos and impressive stories, but when you tie in to a rope and set your anchors, you are sharing an experience with the best climbers in the world.

Appendix 1: Webbing, Cord, and Carabiners

Webbing, cord, and carabiners are used for rigging climbing anchors. It's important to have the right material for the job.

CORD AND WEBBING

Cord is available in nylon and other high-strength materials. With nylon, use at least 7-millimeter-diameter cord for anchoring. This is probably the best material for anchor cordelettes, except that it's a little heavy and bulky. The ultra-high-strength cords are suitable in diameters of 5.5 millimeters. When buying a cordelette, about 4 meters (13 feet) of cord makes a good rescue cord. For building anchors, 5–6 meters (16–20 feet) is a good length.

Webbing comes in nylon and varying thicknesses of Spectra/Dyneema. Nylon grips better for making friction hitches in emergency situations, but the thin Spectra slings are compact and light. Knotted webbing slings are fading in popularity—sewn slings are stronger, less bulky, and cannot accidentally untie.

Soft goods, such as the nylon or Spectra, in cords, slings, harnesses, and ropes are susceptible to gradual weakening from ultraviolet exposure, and even rapid weakening from chemical contamination, especially battery acids. For that reason, you want to take good care of your climbing gear. Don't toss it in a messy car trunk; rather, store it in a dry, dark, clean place.

CARABINERS

Climbers use carabiners for multiple purposes, including

- clipping in to belay and rappel anchors,
- clipping the climbing rope in to lead protection,
- rigging a belay/rappel device,
- carrying equipment on the harness or gear sling,
- connecting gear to the rope for hauling.

CARABINER SHAPE

Carabiners come in many shapes and sizes. A rack of super-light carabiners can save a lot of weight, but some are so small that they're hard to clip. The best ones work great and can slice a good deal of weight from the rack. Many climbers have two sets of carabiners—one set of large biners for working sport climbs and a second set of ultralight biners for long routes and on-sight climbing, where weight matters.

The shape of a carabiner's cross-section helps determine its strength, weight, and the radius of its rope-bearing surface. A smaller radius carabiner can severely stress the climbing rope by bending it too sharply under load. Carabiners with a round cross-section require more mass of aluminum than other carabiner shapes to provide a given strength. An oval cross-section allows a slightly lighter mass to provide the same pulling strength, though you lose some strength if the carabiner is loaded sideways. Modern carabiners with I-shaped, T-shaped, and hourglass cross-sections place the aluminum mass where it provides great strength and an ample rope-bearing surface.

Oval. Oval carabiners work great for racking wired nuts. They put equal loads on the spine and gate, though, so they are weaker than D-shaped or asymmetrical carabiners (because the spine is stronger than the gate). They are also larger and heavier than more modern designs.

D-shape. D-shaped carabiners concentrate the force on the carabiner's spine for increased strength, but most climbers prefer asymmetrical designs.

Asymmetrical. Asymmetrical carabiners put the load on the spine and have a large gate opening for easy clipping. The asymmetrical design allows for smaller, lighter carabiners to be clipped easily as well as having adequate open-gate and cross-load strength. For these reasons, the vast majority of carabiners used today are asymmetrical.

CARABINER STRENGTH

Carabiner spines are stamped with three strength ratings. (If your carabiners are not stamped with strength ratings, retire them and buy new ones.) The following symbols identify the strength ratings:

- ↔ **Closed-gate strength:** A carabiner is by far strongest when loaded along its spine with the gate closed.
- ◯ **Gate-open strength:** A carabiner with its gate open can lose two-thirds or more of its strength. The UIAA minimum for open-gate strength is 7 kN.
- ↕ **Cross-loaded strength:** A cross-loaded carabiner, with the weight pulling outward on the gate, also loses two-thirds or more of its strength.
- Any carabiner may be dangerously weak if leveraged over an edge, and there is no UIAA standard for leveraged-carabiner strength. Take care to ensure carabiners are hanging in their optimal positions and that there is more than one of them between you and disaster.

CARABINER GATE

Carabiners come with several types of gates. A carabiner gate should be easy to clip, and it must provide strength when the carabiner is closed. One end of the carabiner gate has a hinge upon which the gate rotates, and the other end has some sort of closure for connecting the gate to the carabiner when it's closed. This connection is a crucial component of the carabiner's strength—without it, a closed carabiner will be no stronger than a carabiner with its gate open.

Solid gate. For many years, all carabiners came with a straight solid gate, and many excellent modern carabiners still have solid gates. One possible disadvantage of the solid gate is that in a fall, the mass of the gate can cause it to vibrate open and closed. If the load comes onto the carabiner with the gate open, it can break. This is rare, but it occasionally happens.

Bent gate. Bent-gate carabiners make it easier to clip the rope in. Because of the tendency for the bend in the gate to hang up in bolt hangers, holding the carabiner in a compromised position, these carabiners should be used only on the rope ends of quickdraws.

Wire gate. Wire gates are strong, light, easy to clip, and less prone to vibrate in a leader fall, which decreases the chance of breaking a carabiner. Anecdotal evidence suggests they will accidentally unclip more easily than a straight solid gate, but keeping more than one carabiner between you and eternity is a good idea anyway.

Pin-and-notch. Traditionally, the carabiner gate has a pin that closes into a notch in the carabiner. If the carabiner is severely loaded, the pin locks into the notch to provide strength at the gate. The notch sometimes snags on the wire cable of nuts, which can be inconvenient.

Keylock. The keylock gate closure provides a strong, clean closure with no notch to snag on gear, but it can collect snow or dirt on adventurous climbs and prevent the gate from closing entirely.

LOCKING CARABINERS

Locking the gate on a carabiner prevents the gate from accidentally opening and unclipping. Locking carabiners are used for many crucial clipping points, including

- clipping in to anchors,
- rigging belay or rappel devices,
- clipping a haul rope to the harness,
- attaching a pack to a haul rope,
- clipping crucial lead protection.

Shape

Locking carabiners come in a few shapes. The original "lockers" were D-shaped and oval, though now the asymmetrical and pear shapes are more popular. It's nice to carry some small, lightweight locking carabiners for applications that do not require a big gate opening or large interior space. The large pear-shaped HMS locking carabiners work well with a Munter hitch for belaying or rappelling without a device, and their larger size makes them easy to handle. (*HMS* comes from the German *halbmastwurfsicherung*, which means "half clove-hitch belay.")

Gate

Locking carabiners are available in three different gate designs. Which you use depends on your personal preference.

Screw gate. The locking collar spins one way to lock a standard screw-gate carabiner and the opposite way to unlock it. For a secure lock, spin the collar until it cannot spin any farther (not just partway down). Screw-gate carabiners are convenient because you can easily clip them when they're unlocked, but you have to remember to lock them when you need security. Make a habit of locking the gate immediately after clipping it.

Autolocking. Autolocking carabiners have spring-loaded gates that lock automatically whenever the gate closes. They are great for new climbers and those who often forget to lock their carabiners. Some climbers prefer the autolocking feature, while others find it a nuisance when trying to clip the carabiner. It is possible for some autolocking gates to open if a loaded rope runs across them.

Button-lock. Button-locking carabiners lock automatically when you twist the gate. To unlock them, push the button and spin the gate. This design makes it difficult for the carabiner to accidentally unlock, but most climbers don't find it as convenient as a standard screw gate.

CARABINER CARE

Inspect your carabiners periodically. If you find notches or grooves in them (a kind of erosion that results from rappelling or repeated lowering), retire them. Many bolt hangers have sharp edges, which can be hard on carabiners, especially when you are working sport routes. If a carabiner becomes gouged, retire it. If a carabiner gets dropped a long way, toss it out—chances are it's still fine, but you don't want to learn otherwise by taking a huge fall when your carabiner breaks!

If a carabiner gate becomes sticky, lubricate it. Use a Teflon spray lubricant or a lubricant sold for camming devices, because these attract less dirt. If it's still sticky, discard the carabiner—it's dangerous if the gate does not close every time you clip the carabiner.

QUICKDRAWS

Quickdraws are the workhorses of sport climbing equipment. Sport draws ideally have a bent-gate carabiner on the bottom that is sewn tightly to prevent the carabiner from rotating and a straight- or wire-gate carabiner on the top. Many people prefer sport draws to be somewhat stiff for easy clipping, but on long pitches or multipitch routes, and on-sight climbing at your limit, weight is a critical consideration, and the thinner, more flexible webbing may be a better choice. Quickdraws for traditional climbing can be the same sport draws with a few extendable quickdraws tossed in or another set of lighter, more pliable draws. Inspect the webbing for wear and the carabiner for notching (especially the top one that gets gouged by bolt hangers).

Appendix 2: Knots

Climbers use knots for many purposes. This section focuses on knots used by climbers to construct anchor systems and attach themselves to the anchors. Other climbing knots are not included—see *Rock Climbing: Mastering Basic Skills* and *Knots for Climbers*, both by Craig Luebben, or Clyde Soles's *The Outdoor Knots Book* for more climbing knots. Animated, step-by-step guides, such as www.animatedknots.com, can be found online and are excellent resources for reminders and basic instruction on how to tie most knots.

When reading the knot descriptions, the *free end* is the end of the rope, while the *standing end* refers to the side with most of the length of the rope. A *bight* is a loop of rope that does not cross itself, while a *coil* is a loop that does cross itself. When tying knots, keep them tidy and free of extra twists so that they maintain full strength and are easy to visually check.

Some knots weaken the rope more than others because they bend it in a tighter radius. This creates shear stress in the rope (loading across the rope fibers rather than along their length) and can severely stress the rope on the outside edge of the bend. The figure eight is a strong knot for tying in

to rope because it does not bend the rope sharply. Many climbing books include a chart to show the relative strength of various climbing knots. These numbers are only roughly accurate, and they change with the material and diameter of the cord.

KNOTS FOR TYING IN TO THE HARNESS

The tie-in knot is the one we trust our lives to every time we go climbing. It is not redundant, has not benefited from technological improvements to reduce human error, and even if you tie it correctly a thousand times in a row, that one time you do it wrong will probably kill you. Tie your knot without distraction, check your partner's knot, and have them check yours. Every time.

FIGURE-EIGHT TIE-IN

This is the standard knot for tying the rope to your harness because it's strong, secure, and easy to visually check.

A properly tied, well-dressed, and tightly cinched figure-eight knot does not require a backup knot unless the rope is especially stiff. Nonetheless, it's not a bad idea to add a backup to your tie-in knot.

A. Make a figure eight in the rope 2 or 3 feet from the end.

B. Pass the end of the rope through the tie-in points on your harness, which usually include the leg loops and waist belt.

C. Retrace the eight with the end of the rope, starting from where the rope emerges from the harness.

D. Continue retracing the knot so that the second strand lies parallel to the first.

E. Keep the knot tidy, or "well dressed." Avoid extra twists and make the tie-in loop small so that the knot sits close to your harness. Cinch all four rope strands tight to secure the knot.

GRAPEVINE BACKUP

A properly tied figure-eight knot does not need backup, however, many climbers tie a backup knot that protects the primary knot from untying. Some use a simple overhand, but the overhand often unties itself within a single pitch of climbing. Use a grapevine or extra pass to back up your figure-eight knot.

A. Tie a grapevine knot to back up the figure eight. Coil the rope once around its standing end, then cross over the first coil and make a second coil.

B. Pass the rope end through the inside of these coils and cinch the grapevine tight. Leave a 2- or 3-inch (5- or 8-centimeter) tail in the end of the rope.

EXTRA PASS BACKUP

The extra pass is simple: pass the rope end one more time through the figure-eight knot to secure it.

C. Tie a figure-eight knot, then pass the rope end one more time through the figure eight.

D. This secures the figure eight.

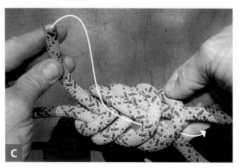

KNOTS FOR TYING IN TO ANCHORS

Always use a locking carabiner for tying in to anchors. Lacking a locking carabiner, you can substitute two carabiners with gates opposed (facing opposite directions).

CLOVE HITCH

The clove hitch allows you to adjust the length of your tie-in to the anchors without untying or unclipping the knot. To extend or shorten your tie-in, simply feed rope through the clove hitch. Once you unclip the clove hitch, it's gone—no knot to untie. Always cinch the clove hitch tight by pulling on both rope strands, otherwise it can loosen and possibly unclip itself from the carabiner.

Forming the two loops and clipping them in to the carabiner is the fastest way to tie the clove hitch. When belaying a lead climber, tie the clove hitch with the load strand next to the spine of the carabiner for maximum strength. The carabiner can lose up to 30 percent of its strength (depending on the carabiner shape and rope diameter) if the load strand sits near the carabiner gate. This is not a problem if the carabiner holds only body weight, but it could be dangerous if the attached belayer catches a leader fall.

A. *Twist two coils into the rope so that it looks like a two-coil spring.*
B. *Slide the top coil below the bottom coil. Do not twist or rotate the coils.*
C. *Clip both coils into a locking carabiner and lock the gate. If you'll be belaying a lead climber, be sure that the load strand of your rope sits next to the spine of the carabiner.*

load strand

OVERHAND

The overhand knot is useful for creating a loop. Because it puts a sharper bend in the rope, it's not quite as strong as a figure-eight knot, and it's harder to untie after being heavily loaded.

A. Take a bight of rope and make a coil in both strands of the bight.

B. Pass the bight through the coil.

C. Cinch the overhand tight.

FIGURE EIGHT ON A BIGHT

Tie a figure eight in the middle of the rope to make a strong loop for clipping yourself in to anchors. The figure eight on a bight works in many situations where you need a secure loop to clip. It is easy to untie even after loading.

A. Take a bight of rope and form a figure eight with the two strands of the bight.
B. Pull the bight through itself, cinch the figure eight tight, and clip it.

DOUBLE-LOOP FIGURE EIGHT

The double-loop figure eight creates two secure loops that can be clipped to two different anchors. It is not truly redundant, because if one loop severs, the other loop may slip through the knot, causing anchor failure. However, the rope is rarely redundant anyway. Make sure the rope does not contact any sharp edges.

A. Begin tying a figure eight on a bight, with a longer than normal loop.

B. Rather than passing the initial bight through the eight to finish the knot, pass a bight from each strand through the figure eight.

C. Take the initial bight and flop it over the entire knot.

D. Pull the resulting bights through the figure eight to cinch the knot tight.

E. Adjust the loop lengths by pulling the rope through the figure eight. This lengthens one loop and shortens the other.

KNOTS FOR TYING A ROPE AROUND A TREE OR BOULDER

DOUBLE BOWLINE

The double bowline is great for tying a rope around a tree, boulder, or other natural anchor. Many sport climbers also use a double bowline for tying in because it's a snap to untie, even after multiple falls. A loosely tied double bowline can untie itself if the knot is wiggled, especially if the rope is stiff—always back up the double bowline with a grapevine or other secure backup knot and cinch both knots tight.

A. Pass the rope around a tree or other anchor, then twist two coils in the standing end of the rope.

B. Bring the free end of the rope up through the coils, down around the standing end of the rope, and back down through the coils. The rope's free end should come into the middle of the double bowline.

C. Cinch the double bowline tight.

D. Finish the bowline with a grapevine backup.

KNOTS FOR JOINING WEBBING OR CORD

While sewn webbing has reduced the need for tying knots in slings, it is still essential to know how to tie the ends of cord or webbing.

WATER KNOT

Water knots tie pieces of webbing into loops. The water knot unties over time as it gets loaded and unloaded—check that the tails are at least 7 or 8 centimeters (3 inches) long every time you climb. Some climbers tape the tails to prevent them from creeping. If you do this, leave the ends of the webbing in view so you can see them.

A. Tie an overhand knot in one end of a sling and match the other end of the webbing to the first end.
B. Retrace the original overhand knot.
C. Cinch the knot tight. The tails should be at least 8 centimeters (3 inches) long.

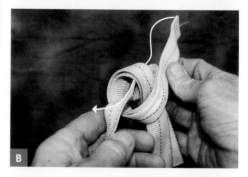

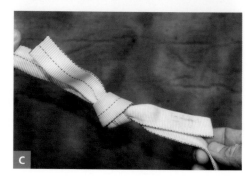

FLAT OVERHAND

Many guides use the flat overhand for tying a cordelette into a loop because it's quick to tie and untie. The flat overhand is more secure than it appears, provided that you cinch it super tight and leave the tails at least 30 centimeters (12 inches) long.

A. Take both ends together and tie an overhand knot.

B. Cinch the knot tight, leaving a tail at least 30 centimeters (12 inches) long.

C. If the ropes are icy or dramatically different diameters or types (such as one dynamic and one static), adding a second knot, as shown, will increase the strength and security of the knot.

D. This rope is now ready for rappelling.

DOUBLE FISHERMAN'S

The double fisherman's knot joins cord into a loop, for example, to close a cordelette or sling a chock.

A. Coil one free end of the cord around the other.

B. Cross the cord over itself and make a second coil.

C. Pass the end through the inside of the coils.

D. Repeat the first step, this time coiling the second rope around the first, but in the opposite direction so that the finished knots are parallel to each other.

E. Cinch the knots tight. When the knot is finished, the coils should be clean and parallel as shown.

HITCHES

A hitch is a knot that requires the application of force in order to retain its structure. Hitches are among the most versatile of climbing techniques, and the following hitches are mandatory techniques for any climber to know.

GIRTH HITCH

The girth hitch has many uses. With it, you can

- fasten a sling or daisy chain to your harness for clipping in to anchors (always tie in to anchors with the climbing rope if you will be belaying),
- fasten a sling around a tree to make an anchor,
- attach two slings together to make them longer,
- connect a sling to a carabiner without opening the carabiner's gate (perhaps because it's your only attachment to the anchor).

Don't girth-hitch the cable on a nut or chock or any other small-diameter object, because the sling may be cut by it under load.

In a recent incident, a thin Spectra/Dyneema sling that was girth-hitched to another sling broke under little more than body weight. The sling may have been compromised, but climbers may wish to avoid girth-hitching slings of different diameters together. If shock loading is anticipated, use a carabiner attachment instead of a girth hitch.

A. *Pass the webbing sling through your belay loop or around any object you want to fasten it to, and pull one end of the webbing through itself to create the hitch.*
B. *This fastens the webbing to the belay loop. Consider adding a second piece of webbing for redundancy.*

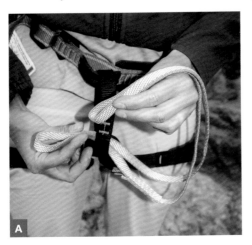

PRUSIK

The prusik is a friction hitch, and if you're going to learn to use only one friction hitch, the prusik is it. It's easy to remember, and it grips well.

A. Take a thin-diameter cord (5–7 millimeters in diameter) tied into a loop, wrap it once around both strands of the rappel rope, and pass it through itself as if you're making a girth hitch.

B. Wrap the cord once again around the rope and through itself.

C. Now you have a 2-wrap prusik.

D. Repeat the procedure to create a 3-wrap prusik for more friction. Keep the wraps neat and parallel.

AUTOBLOCK

The autoblock adds convenience and safety by backing up your brake hand when rappelling. If you accidentally let go of the rope, the autoblock "grabs" the rope and halts your descent. The autoblock prevents overheating your brake hand on a long, steep rappel, because your hand rests on the autoblock, not the sliding ropes.

The autoblock is usually set on the harness leg loop so that it cannot touch the belay/rappel device. If the autoblock tails are too long, or if the rappel device sits too low, the cord can touch the device. In this case, it may not lock, or worse, it could jam in your rappel device, stranding you until you unweight it. If you can't get the required separation between your autoblock and rappel device, extend the rappel device farther from your harness by girth-hitching two short slings in to your belay loop and attaching the rappel device to them.

B. Wrap it four times until you have a 5- to 7.5-centimeter (2- to 3-inch) tail on each end.

A. Clip a nylon sling or a loop of cord to your leg loop with a locking carabiner. Wrap the sling or cord around the rope. To shorten the resulting knot, you can also girth-hitch one end of the sling or cord to your leg loop, then clip the other with a carabiner.

C. Wrap the cord too tight, and you'll have a slow, jerky rappel; not tight enough, and the autoblock won't grab when you need it. Practice with the autoblock to get the length right. The rappel device goes on the rope above the autoblock.

227

Appendix 3: Equations

We omitted scientific equations in the text to make the discussion of climbing physics less confusing. The following equations relate to material in chapter 10, Climbing Forces.

$F = ma$

F = force
m = mass
a = acceleration

$W = mg$

W = weight
g = acceleration due to gravity (which is constant at the earth's surface)

$E_p = mgh$

E_p = potential energy
h = height (length of a potential fall)

$E_K = \frac{1}{2}mv^2$

E_K = kinetic energy
v = velocity

$P = mv$

P = momentum

$I = P_{initial} - P_{final}$

I = impulse
$P_{initial}$ = momentum before the rope begins to arrest the fall
$P_{final} = 0$ (momentum after the fall has been arrested)

$I = m(v_{max}-v_{final})$

v_{max} = maximum falling velocity
$v_{final} = 0$ (velocity after fall has been stopped)

$v_{max} = (2gh)^{\frac{1}{2}}$

the potential energy at the beginning of a free fall equals the kinetic energy as the rope begins to arrest the fall, which allows us to calculate the maximum velocity of the falling climber

$I = m(2gh)^{\frac{1}{2}}$

the impulse required to arrest a fall is determined by the falling climber's mass and the length of the fall

Opposite: *An old guide once said, "It's okay to challenge your ability with the equipment, or your ability with the climbing, but never both at the same time."*

Glossary

aid climbing Pulling on protection or climbing upward while standing in slings attached to anchors. Aid climbing is used to bypass sections that the team cannot free-climb.

American Triangle A dangerous anchor-rigging method that increases the force on the individual anchors. It is created by threading the webbing or cord through two anchors and tying the ends together, forming a triangle that causes the anchors to pull against each other; the larger the angle in the triangle's bottom corner, the greater the forces. This technique is dangerous if the anchors are not bomber; it was popular before the forces were well understood and can still occasionally be found on fixed rappel anchors.

AMGA American Mountain Guides Association is a national nonprofit organization that promotes high standards for guides. AMGA trains and certifies guides in rock guiding, alpine guiding, and ski mountaineering guiding and accredits guiding companies.

anchor Any temporary or permanent attachment to the rock used to protect a climber against a fall, fix a team to a belay, or fix a rappel rope. A good anchor can hold several thousand pounds, a bad anchor may crumple under body weight. Anchors come in many forms, including trees, boulders, chockstones, pitons, bolts, nuts, hexagonal chocks, camming devices, expandable tubes, and more.

assisted-braking belay device A belay device that will lock on to the rope under the force of a fall and does not rely on the squeezing action of the belayer's hand to initiate and sustain the hold on the rope, although it is still recommended that the belayer maintain brake hand control of the rope when using this device.

auto-belay system A mechanical belay common in climbing gyms that allows the climber to ascend the wall with a top-ropelike belay from above and lower back to the ground without needing a partner. Auto-belay systems use webbing

Opposite: *Topher Donahue on the bivy during the first ascent of* Air Guitar *(5.12+), Black Canyon of the Gunnison, Colorado*

and either centrifugal force or magnets to slowly lower a climber's weight the moment the webbing is weighted.

autoblock A friction hitch that is commonly used to provide a backup for rappelling or lowering, but it can also be used to ascend a fixed rope.

autoblocking belay device A belay device that can be configured to belay a second climber in a manner that locks the rope automatically in a fall.

autolocking carabiner A carabiner with a spring-loaded gate that locks automatically when you close the gate.

back-clip Clipping the rope backward through a protection carabiner so that the rope runs through the carabiner toward the rock. This increases the chance that the rope could snap across the gate and accidentally unclip.

belay Managing the rope to protect a climber, catch him if he falls, hold him if he hangs, and lower him when it's time to come down, aided by the friction of the belay device; also refers to belay station.

belay anchor An anchor, usually multi-point, that the team uses to secure a belay station.

belay device A device that creates sharp bends in the rope to provide friction for belaying or rappelling.

belay loop A sewn loop on the front of all good rock climbing harnesses. The loop is most commonly used for clipping the belay or rappel device to a climber and is sometimes used to connect the climber to an anchor system.

bent-gate carabiner A carabiner with its gate bent inward for easy rope clipping.

beta Information about moves, protection, strategy, or other knowledge—given either before or during the ascent—that may help a climber ascend a route.

bight Any bend in the rope that does not cross itself. A bight is used for creating many knots and to thread the rope in to belay/rappel devices.

big wall A tall cliff that normally requires multiple days to ascend.

bolt An anchor consisting of a metal bolt that is either set in a drilled hole and expands in the hole when tightened (creating friction that secures the bolt in place) or is glued in to the hole with epoxy; an accompanying hanger provides an attachment point for clipping a carabiner. Well-placed bolts that are 10 millimeters (⅜ inch) or more in diameter are suitable for rock climbing anchors; smaller-diameter bolts should be considered dangerous.

bombproof Describes a completely reliable anchor; also called *bomber*.

bouldering Climbing without a rope, usually close to the ground where a fall does not have bad consequences.

cam A common term for a spring-loaded camming device; also refers to the individual camming lobes in a camming device. *Cam* can also be used as a verb when a downward force is dispersed into a crack wall as an outward force, creating friction to oppose the downward pull.

carabiner A high-strength aluminum snap-link used to connect parts of a climbing system.

chock Term for an artificial chockstone—a climbing anchor that wedges in a constriction for security, including hexagonal chocks and nuts.

chockstone A stone wedged in a crack.

cleaning Removing protection anchors from a climb.

clove hitch A hitch used for tying a rope in to an anchor or connecting some gear to the rope. A clove hitch is often used by the climber to clip in to the belay anchors because it is easy to adjust the tie-in length.

coil A bend in rope or webbing that crosses over itself.

cord Round accessory cord up to 7 millimeters in diameter and made of high-strength materials; used for cordelettes, slinging chocks, and making short loops.

cordelette A 5- to 7.5-meter (16- to 25-foot) piece of cord, usually between 5.5 millimeters and 7 millimeters in diameter and often tied into a loop. A cordelette is used in many tasks, including building belay anchors and aiding in self-rescue.

crux The hardest move or series of moves on a pitch; the hardest pitch on a multi-pitch climb.

double fisherman's knot A standard knot for joining two ropes together or for tying a piece of cord into a loop.

double-length sling A sling that, when folded in half, fits nicely over the climber's shoulder.

dynamic belay A technique in which the belayer intentionally lets some rope slip through the belay device in a leader fall to decrease the impact force on the climber and anchors.

dynamic rope A climbing rope that stretches under load to absorb the kinetic energy of a falling climber without allowing the impact force to become so great as to injure the climber or break the anchors.

dyno A dynamic move, where the climber pushes on the footholds and pulls on the handholds to gain momentum, then flies upward to catch a faraway hold.

equalize Tying the anchors together so they share any load; ideally they share it equally.

ERNEST An acronym for a set of principles for constructing belay anchors: Equalized, Redundant, No Extension, Solid, and Timely.

extension A potential extension of slings or cords in an anchor system caused by failure of a single point. An extension can create a higher impact force on the remaining anchors.

fall factor A measure of the severity of a fall, calculated by dividing the length of the fall by the length of rope in the system. The greater the fall factor, the greater the impact force on the anchors, climber, and belayer.

figure-eight knot A knot that is shaped like a numeral eight; used for tying the rope in to the harness, tying two ropes together, tying a loop for clipping in to anchors, connecting a haul pack to the rope, and so on.

fixed protection Any permanent anchor point; usually a bolt, piton, or permanently set chock or cam.

four-cam unit A camming unit with four cam lobes. A four-cam unit is often stronger than a three-cam unit.

free-soloing Climbing a route without a rope. When free-soloing, a fall can be, and often is, fatal.

friction hitch Any of several hitches that will lock on to the rope when loaded yet can be slid along the rope when not loaded; most often used for self-rescue techniques.

gate flutter The fast, repeated opening and closing of a carabiner gate that can occur when the rope runs through it during a fall.

girth hitch A hitch used to connect a sling or loop of cord to an object by wrapping it around the object and through itself.

GriGri An assisted-braking belay device made by Petzl.

half rope A rope designed to be used in pairs, but the individual ropes can be clipped in separately to protection points to reduce rope drag.

hand crack A crack the right size for setting hand jams.

hanging belay A belay stance with no ledge, so the climbers must hang in their harnesses.

hexagonal chock An asymmetrical, six-sided chock that wedges in to three different sizes of cracks.

hitch A type of knot where a rope or cord fastens around an object; without the object, the hitch would come undone.

HMS carabiner A large pear-shaped carabiner that works great with a Munter hitch.

horn A spike of rock that can be used for an anchor or hold.

impact force The peak load developed in a leader fall; the force is greatest on the top anchor.

kilonewton (kN) A metric measurement of force. One kilonewton is equal to about 225 pounds of force.

lap coil A method of stacking the rope back and forth over the belayer's tie-in at hanging belays.

lap link An open steel ring with overlapping ends that are hammered together after the ring is placed around something. A lap link is often used to connect rappel ropes to fixed rappel anchors and is sometimes used as a lowering ring on sport routes.

lead climbing Climbing first up a pitch and placing protection as you go.

leader The person leading a pitch or climb.

lead fall A fall taken while leading; the leader falls twice the distance to the last piece of protection.

locking carabiner A carabiner with a gate that locks closed to prevent it from accidentally opening.

lock off Holding the body in position with one arm while the other arm reaches for the next hold or high protection.

lowering Descending by hanging on the rope and being lowered by the belayer.

This is the common method of descent from a slingshot top rope or sport climb.

master point The main attachment loop in a belay or rappel anchor.

multidirectional anchor An anchor that can hold a load in any direction.

multipitch route A route that must be climbed in multiple pitches with intermediate belays.

Munter hitch A hitch that creates friction on the rope; used for belaying and rappelling.

natural protection An anchor made from a natural feature, such as a tree, boulder, chockstone, horn, or rock tunnel.

nut Term for a wedge-shaped anchor that locks into constrictions in a crack to create an anchor.

nut tool A thin metal pick used to help loosen and remove stuck protection or to clean cracks.

objective hazard A hazard that cannot be controlled by the climber; for example, rockfall, lightning, weather.

off-width crack A crack that is too wide for fists and too small to fit the body; one of the more difficult and despised types of climbing.

on-sight To lead a route on the first try without falling or hanging on the rope and without any prior knowledge about the moves, strategy, or protection; this is the finest style in which to ascend a route.

opposition Using anchors in opposition to each other to create a multidirectional anchor.

overhanging A section of rock that is steeper than vertical.

pitch The section of a climb between belays; a pitch climbs from one belay station to the next.

piton A steel spike that is hammered into a crack to create an anchor; an eye on the piton provides an attachment point. Pitons are fixed in place on some traditional routes that might be hard to protect with nuts and cams, and fixed pitons may or may not be reliable anchors.

pocket A hole in the rock that forms a hand- or foothold and sometimes a place to set protection.

protection point A rock anchor that a leader clips the rope to for safety if a fall occurs; often called *pro*.

prusik A friction hitch used in self-rescue systems. A prusik creates the highest friction of all the friction knots included in this book.

pulley effect The potential doubling of the impact force on the top anchor because it must hold the force of the falling climber *and* the force of the belayer.

quickdraw A short sling with a carabiner clipped to each end that is used for connecting the rope to bolts and nuts or for extending the protection on an anchor to minimize bending of the rope.

rack The collection of protection anchors, slings, quickdraws, etc. that climbers carry up a route to build the protection system.

rappel A method used for descending a rope in order to return to the ground.

rappel anchor Any anchor used to hold the rope when rappelling.

rappel backup A friction hitch used to back up the brake hand when rappelling.

rappel device A device, also used for belaying, that creates friction on the rope so a climber can control the rappel.

rappel ring A metal ring, preferably steel, attached to a fixed anchor; the rope is threaded through the ring (usually two or more rings attached to two or more anchors) to anchor the rope for rappelling or lowering.

redirect Changing the direction of pull on a rope by rerouting it through an anchor. This technique is often used to run the climber's rope up to a high anchor and back to the belayer, thereby decreasing the load on the belayer and pulling the belayer up rather than down.

redpoint To climb a route without falling after previous effort spent working out the moves.

redundant Relying on more than a single link in the protection system; if a single point fails, one or more backups exist.

rest position Any body position that takes weight off the arms for a rest.

rockfall Rocks falling from above as a result of either natural or human causes; this is an objective hazard that climbers need to be aware of and avoid.

rope bag A nylon sack used to carry and protect the rope.

rope drag Friction caused by the rope running over the rock and through carabiners. Rope drag increases with each bend in the rope.

rope tarp A fabric mat for stacking the rope on the ground. To move to another route, you roll up the tarp, move it, and unroll the tarp without having to coil the rope; this is extremely convenient when climbing multiple single-pitch routes.

runout A section on a climb with a long distance between protection points, either because the protection was not available or because the climber chose not to set it.

sandbag To mislead a climber regarding the difficulty or danger of a route; sandbagging is not cool, because it can be dangerous.

screw gate A locking carabiner that locks shut when the gate is turned a few rotations.

second The climber who follows the leader up a pitch, cleaning the protection as he or she goes, with a top rope from the leader for safety.

seconding The act of following on a climb and cleaning a pitch.

self-rescue The act of rescuing your own team in the event of a mishap, using only the standard climbing equipment that you are carrying.

sheath The woven nylon outer layer of a rope that protects the core.

shock load The impact resulting from failure of one piece that causes the load to drop onto another, or any time a fall is held by material less dynamic than the climbing rope, such as onto webbing or static cord.

shoulder sling A piece of webbing sewn or tied into a loop, just long enough to comfortably fit over the climber's shoulder.

simul-belay The act of belaying two climbers who follow a pitch at the same time; this technique is sometimes used by advanced climbers or guides for a team of three.

single rope A dynamic climbing rope rated to be used by itself for protecting a lead climber or second.

slab A rock face that is less than vertical.

slings Webbing sewn or tied into a loop; typically shoulder length to triple-shoulder length.

slingshot top rope The most common system for top-roping: the rope passes from the climber, up to the anchors at the top of the route, and back down to the belayer who is stationed on the ground.

sport climbing Climbing where all the protection consists of fixed bolts. Sport climbing routes are usually single-pitch routes, where the climber is lowered back to the ground after completing the climb.

squeeze chimney A chimney just wide enough to barely admit the climber's body.

stacking the rope Uncoiling the rope in to a loose pile with the top and bottom ends exposed; the leader ties in to the top end. Stacking minimizes tangles; also called flaking the rope.

static elongation The amount a rope will stretch when holding a body-weight load.

static rope A climbing rope that stretches little so it works great for hauling,

top-roping, or ascending a fixed line, but it is not suitable for lead climbing.

stemming Using footholds in opposition to get weight off the hands and to increase the security of marginal footholds; often used in inside corners.

stick-clip To clip the rope to the first bolt on a route by attaching a carabiner or quickdraw to a long stick. This technique prevents a ground fall if the climber falls in the beginning of the route.

stopper knot A knot tied in the end of a rope to keep a climber from rappelling or being lowered off the end of the rope.

subjective hazard A hazard that usually can be controlled by good judgment or conservatism on the part of the climber.

tail The rope end that sticks out after tying a knot.

thread Any naturally occurring tunnel in the rock that a sling may be passed through to create an anchor.

three-cam unit A camming unit with three cams. A three-cam unit is often weaker than a four-cam unit but fits into shallow cracks. Also known as a TCU.

topo A map of a route that uses symbols to show the rock features, belays, and fixed protection.

top-rope anchor The belay anchor for a top rope.

top-rope fall A fall while climbing on a top rope. The fall is usually very short unless there is slack in the system.

traditional (trad) climbing Climbing a route where the leader sets protection points along the way to be removed later by the second (as opposed to sport climbing).

transition The steps required to change from one climbing system to another; for example, from climbing to rappelling.

traverse A section on a climb or boulder problem that moves sideways rather than up.

tri-axial loading A situation where a carabiner is pulled in three directions, weakening the carabiner.

Tricam An anchor that can be wedged into a constriction in a crack or cammed into a parallel crack. Tricams are extremely versatile but not always stable.

triple-length sling A sling that, when folded into thirds, fits nicely over a climber's shoulder.

twin ropes Thin ropes that must be used in pairs, with both ropes clipped in to all protection points; this provides two ropes for rappelling.

UIAA The Union Internationale des Associations d'Alpinisme is the international association of national climbing clubs that sets standards for and tests climbing safety equipment. Also known as the International Climbing and Mountaineering Federation.

walking The tendency for camming units to move in the crack when wriggled by the climbing rope. Walking can compromise the placement, though this is often negated by clipping the rope in with a long extension.

water knot The standard knot for tying webbing into a loop; a retraced overhand knot.

webbing Nylon fibers woven flat like a strap; used for making slings.

wedge To lock a chock or nut into place in a constricting section of a crack.

wire-gate carabiner A carabiner with a gate made of wire instead of solid-aluminum stock. A wire-gate carabiner decreases weight and minimizes the chance of having the gate vibrate open in a fall, which can cause the carabiner to break.

Resources

Access Fund: P.O. Box 17010, Boulder, CO 80308; (303) 545-6772; www.accessfund.org

American Alpine Club: 710 Tenth Street, Suite 100, Golden, CO 80401; (303) 384-0110; www.americanalpineclub.org

American Mountain Guides Association: 4720 Walnut Street, #200 Boulder, CO 80301; (303) 271-0984; www.amga.com

Leave No Trace: P.O. Box 997, Boulder, CO 80306; (303) 442-8222; www.lnt.org

The International Climbing and Mountaineering Federation (UIAA, Union Internationale des Associations d'Alpinisme): www.theuiaa.org

The Mountaineers: 7700 Sand Point Way NE, Seattle, WA 98115;(206) 521-6001; www.mountaineers.org

CLIMBING WEBSITES

www.alpinist.com
www.climbing.com
www.cubaclimbing.com
www.johngill.net
www.mountainproject.com
www.neclimbs.com
www.neice.com
www.newenglandbouldering.com
www.planetmountain.com
www.redriverclimbing.com
www.rockandice.com
www.rockclimbing.com
www.supertopo.com

Index

Opposite: *Heidi Wirtz demonstrating how to keep the rope running straight and minimize rope drag by placing gear in a straight line even when the cracks and the climb wander, on* Arapilumps *(5.11+), Lumpy Ridge, Colorado*

Opposite: *As long as the gear below is solid and the fall is clean, the leader can venture into the unknown with confidence; but when either of those two factors is in question, climbing gets very dangerous indeed.*

About the Authors

Craig Luebben started guiding and instructing rock and ice climbing in 1981 and became one of America's premier climbing teachers and authors of the climbing craft before his death in a glacial collapse during an unseasonably warm alpine season in the Cascades in 2009. He was an American Mountain Guides Association certified rock guide and taught rock guide courses for the AMGA. He designed Big Bro expandable tube chocks as a mechanical engineering student at Colorado State University; while testing the Big Bro chocks, he became a specialist in off-width cracks. For over twenty years, he studied and tested climbing anchor systems.

He was a senior contributing editor for *Climbing* magazine and has written the instructional books *Knots for Climbers*, *Advanced Rock Climbing* (with John Long), *How to Ice Climb*, *How to Rappel*, *Betty and the Silver Spider: An Introduction to Gym Climbing*, and *Rock Climbing: Mastering Basic Skills*.

Craig opened new rock and ice routes across the United States and in Canada, Mexico, Cuba, France, Italy, Greece, China, and Madagascar. He climbed numerous wall routes in Yosemite Valley, Zion Canyon, and Black Canyon of the Gunnison, and cragged at hundreds of other areas. He is survived by his wife, Silvia, and daughter, Giulia.

Topher Donahue began climbing as a child with his mountain guide father, Mike Donahue. As a young climber back in the day when it wasn't cool to be a young climber, Topher watched climbing evolve from a fringe activity into a mainstream pursuit. He worked as a climbing guide from the time he was a teenager until he took a hiatus from guiding to pursue a career in adventure photojournalism and visit the world's most beautiful climbing areas.

Craig Luebben was a climbing partner and mentor to Topher, and to help keep Craig's books current, Topher wrote the second edition of this title as well as the second edition of Craig Luebben's *Rock Climbing: Mastering Basic Skills*.

Growing up with numerous guides as climbing partners, attending guide trainings starting in elementary school, and then studying journalism in college, Topher developed a unique ability to communicate the finer points of climbing technique to beginner and expert climbers alike. He has also written *Advanced Rock Climbing: Expert Skills and Techniques*, also published by Mountaineers Books; *Bugaboo Dreams: A Story of Skiers, Helicopters & Mountains*; and *Designed by Adventure: 30 Years of Outdoor Research*. He lives in Nederland, Colorado, with his wife and twin son and daughter.

MORE FROM MOUNTAINEERS BOOKS

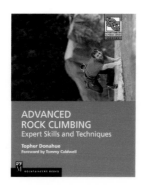

Advanced Rock Climbing
Topher Donahue
*For skilled climbers ready to take it to the next level * Tips and advice from Tommy Caldwell, Steph Davis, Lynn Hill, Alex Honnold and more*

Climbing Self-Rescue
Molly Loomis and Andy Tyson
Techniques for rock, snow, and ice with an emphasis on accident analysis and how to improvise with gear

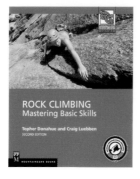

Rock Climbing, 2nd edition
Topher Donahue and Craig Luebben
*For climbers just starting to master basic skills * National Outdoor Book Award*

1001 Climbing Tips
Andy Kirkpatrick
*Bold, irreverent, useful * Winner, best guide-book of the 2006 Banff Mountain Film Festival*

Mountaineering: The Freedom of the Hills, 9th edition
The Mountaineers
Guiding readers to the mountains since 1960

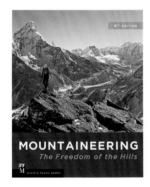

Yoga for Climbers
Nicole Tsong
Prevent injuries and improve your climbing with easy-to-use poses and sequences

MOUNTAINEERS BOOKS

SKIPSTONE   BRAIDED RIVER

recreation · lifestyle · conservation

MOUNTAINEERS BOOKS is a leading publisher of mountaineering literature and guides—including our flagship title, *Mountaineering: The Freedom of the Hills*—as well as adventure narratives, natural history, and general outdoor recreation. Through our two imprints, Skipstone and Braided River, we also publish titles on sustainability and conservation. We are committed to supporting the environmental and educational goals of our organization by providing expert information on human-powered adventure, sustainable practices at home and on the trail, and preservation of wilderness.

The Mountaineers, founded in 1906, is a 501(c)(3) nonprofit outdoor recreation and conservation organization whose mission is to enrich lives and communities by helping people "explore, conserve, learn about, and enjoy the lands and waters of the Pacific Northwest and beyond." One of the largest such organizations in the United States, it sponsors classes and year-round outdoor activities throughout the Pacific Northwest, including climbing, hiking, backcountry skiing, snowshoeing, camping, kayaking, sailing, and more. The Mountaineers also supports its mission through its publishing division, Mountaineers Books, and promotes environmental education and citizen engagement. For more information, visit The Mountaineers Program Center, 7700 Sand Point Way NE, Seattle, WA 98115-3996; phone 206-521-6001; www.mountaineers.org; or email info@mountaineers.org.

Our publications are made possible through the generosity of donors and through sales of more than 800 titles on outdoor recreation, sustainable lifestyle, and conservation. To donate, purchase books, or learn more, visit us online:

MOUNTAINEERS BOOKS

1001 SW Klickitat Way, Suite 201 • Seattle, WA 98134

800-553-4453 • mbooks@mountaineersbooks.org • www.mountaineersbooks.org

An independent nonprofit publisher since 1960

Mountaineers Books is proud to support the Leave No Trace Center for Outdoor Ethics, whose mission is to promote and inspire responsible outdoor recreation through education, research, and partnerships. The Leave No Trace program is focused specifically on human-powered (nonmotorized) recreation. For more information, visit www.lnt.org.